UNCENSORED CONVERSATIONS

A PRACTICAL GUIDE FOR LIVING FROM THE PROVERBS

WORD SPLASH
(RAW, SENSIBLE, PRACTICAL, UNCUT, SIMPLISTIC, UNRESTRICTED, COMMON SENSE APPROACH, THOUGHT-PROVOKING, HONEST)

By
John H. Wooden, MS, Ed.S
Senior Pastor of St. Paul M. B. Church

Printed in the United States of America

ISBN: 978-1-0879-1213-4

10 9 8 7 6 5 4 3 2 1

EMPIRE PUBLISHING
www.empirebookpublishing.com

All Scripture quotations in this book are taken from the New Living Translation of the Bible.

Page layout by author- John H. Wooden

UNCENSORED CONVERSATIONS – A PRACTICAL GUIDE FOR LIVING FROM THE PROVERBS was birthed into my spirit during COVID-19. It is a morning devotional consisting of the Word and Prayer.

DEDICATION

I dedicate this book to the loving memory of my mother, Mrs. Willie Mae Wooden. She was my first teacher and poured wisdom into my life that has defined and shaped my future.

This book is dedicated to my wife, Deborah Ann Wooden, who has been my UNWAVERING ROCK!

I dedicate this book to my two lovely daughters, La'Shannon and Chelsea, and my caring sister, Emma. You ladies have been constant sources of support and strength throughout your entire lives.

I dedicate this book to my handsome grandson, Landon. He will positively impact the world!

I dedicate this book to the Saint Paul Missionary Baptist Church Family. The heart I have for the people within the ministry has prompted the publication of this book.

I dedicate this book to my friend, Letitia Austin, who has constantly encouraged me to put my writings into print.

Finally, I dedicate this book to all persons who have impacted me throughout my life's journey. My life has been enriched because our paths crossed.

FORWARD

UNCENSORED CONVERSATIONS was birthed in my spirit during COVID-19.

My devotional period is usually around 6 AM daily. While resting in bed one morning, I was led to invite others into my personal prayer/devotional time as I listened to the anxieties, frustrations, and daily struggles people were facing during this difficult PANDEMIC.

The Conference Call Devotional was initiated on March 18, 2020 with only me and three additional callers the first week I implemented the process. The Conference Call now ministers to approximately 30 to 50 callers daily. Individuals join the calls for 15 Minutes for a **WORD OF EMPOWERMENT** and **DAILY PRAYER.**

Participants on the calls repeatedly share **prayer requests** and **praise reports** via my FACEBOOK INBOX or through personal text messages. The callers are constantly sending messages concerning how their prayers are being answered and about the strength they are gaining for their daily journeys.

The morning callers have become like family to each other. Our greetings are very personal and genuine. Our concerns for each other are very heartfelt.

This book is filled with **sensible, life-changing, guiding practices** that could literally EMPOWER an individual if the principles and teaching are implemented with fidelity.

It is a simple quick read filled with **POWER-PACKED NUGGETS**. You will not hear this kind of **UNRESTRICTED**

PREACHING and TEACHING from most pulpits. The CONVERSATIONS are RAW and UNCENSORED.

The book addresses an array of topics that will intrigue the readers. POOR DECISION-MAKING can debilitate us. However, wholesome decision making can EQUIP us for life. The book is designed to captivate the attention of every age group. It speaks to our need to believe in ourselves, to financially plan for our future, to be selective of persons we allow into our circles, to challenge us to develop a contingency plan for hard times, and to encourage us to exercise wisdom throughout the course of our lives.

The book provides information about candid conversations parents need to have with their children. It addresses honest conversations that will add strength to relationships. It truly speaks to an unlimited number of areas within our lives.

Many individuals are broken because they have made careless and reckless decisions throughout the course of their lives. The principles provided in this book are designed to help us AVOID DEVASTATING PITFALLS.

People who live CLOSED-MINDED will not be intrigued by this book. However, those who are seeking a MORE PRODUCTIVE WAY OF LIFE will embrace this book to the fullest.

It is a "MUST SHARE" with yourself, your children, your relatives, friends, and coworkers. It is a book filled with WISDOM.

As you read it, bless others by sharing the PRINCIPLES taught throughout the course of the book. If the teachings of this book are applied daily, individuals will discover they can have a richer and more meaningful way of life.

The book will raise a sense of AWARENESS about our PERSONAL RESPONSIBILITY towards SELF! This book is designed to SPEAK LIFE INTO ITS READERS!

As you read the book, you will **laugh, cry, reflect, challenge your own thinking** and face a lot of "**AH HAH MOMENTS!**"

It is my prayer for each reader to be **EMPOWERED, ENCOURAGED, ENLIGHTENED, REFRESHED,** and **INFORMED**.

A PERSONAL NOTETAKING SECTION is intentionally provided at the end of each chapter affording you an opportunity to write down impactful information from your reading.

Allow this book to become a **personal journal** for you. **Allow it to feed your soul. EAT WELL as you peruse through each page. You are guaranteed to become a BETTER YOU.**

Not only will you be blessed by the scriptures provided, but throughout the book, I often share some of my personal experiences with you. I also allow you to hear some of the conversations shared between me and my **first teacher-my mother**, the deceased Mrs. Willie Mae Wooden.

UNCENSORED CONVERSATIONS will be a MIND-BLOWING EXPERIENCE for many of you because it is going to make what you thought were **irrelevant, obsolete**, and **inapplicable** pages of the bible come alive in a manner that is **RELATABLE, PRACTICAL,** and **USER-FRIENDLY!**

Get this book into the hands of every person you love and desire to succeed in life. It is written with **intelligence, passion, love, concern**, and **wisdom**.

I love you and pray you will NEVER BE THE SAME as the HOLY SPIRIT SPEAKS INTO YOUR HEARTS.

Table of Contents

Chapter 1
STOP FLATTERING ME
(JUST TELL ME THE TRUTH)

Proverbs 28:23- *"In the end, people appreciate frankness more than flattery."*

One of the greatest areas of struggle for most of us is that of being candid, frank, and totally honest with people. Oftentimes we know we are being prompted to pour the TRUTH into another person's life, but we withhold the truth for the following reasons:

- We are afraid the other person will get offended.
- We are afraid we might strain the friendship or relationship.
- We are afraid the other person may take what we say the wrong way.
- We are afraid we could possibly lose the friendship.

However, we must understand individuals cannot be helped unless they are exposed to the truth about themselves.

Some people IMPEDE themselves in life.
- They have poor and distasteful attitudes.
- They come across as being A KNOW- IT-ALL!
- They come across as being PUSHY!
- They SHUT their ears to sound advice.
- They fail to EMBRACE the ideas of others.
- They degrade other people privately and publicly.
- They only view life through their own lenses.
- They blame others for their downfalls.

- They fail to see their own contributions to their DESTRUCTIVE DEMISE.

TRUTH is not always a pretty pill to swallow, but when it is delivered delicately, it could be LIFE-CHANGING.

WE HAVE FIVE APPROACHES TO EMPLOY WHEN CONVEYING THE TRUTH TO OTHERS.

Let's briefly discuss five approaches with the final being the most effective. Whenever we are addressing our spouse, our children, our friends, our co-workers, or just people in general, we must be aware of the approaches that will not work.

THE GETTING UP IN YOUR FACE APPROACH- No one enjoys their private space being invaded. Stay at least at arm's length.

THE SCREAMING and HOLLERING APPROACH- We often think the louder we say something, the more effective we are in communicating our position. Yelling and screaming are ABSOLUTE TURNOFFS. Maintain a very low tone.

THE SHAME YOU, BLAME YOU APPROACH- Embarrassing another person should be avoided at all cost. Jesus modeled this practice for us when He dealt with a woman who had been caught in the very act of adultery (John 8:1-11). He waited until He got her alone to discuss her sinful condition.

THE PULLING DOWN THE SHADE APPROACH and LOOKING THE OTHER WAY- Avoidance is not the answer.

We cannot afford to look the other way. Even if it is uncomfortable for us to address the truth with a person, just think about the damage being done when we are not honest with other people.

THE LOVE APPROACH-Approaching people in love is the best approach and it will yield the greatest results. When people are addressed in love, they are usually more receptive to the conversation.

Whenever the truth is shared with individuals, they may initially get upset. However, when they realize you approached them out of genuine concern, they will end up respecting you.

I give people PERMISSION TO SPEAK INTO MY LIFE.
- If you see me heading down a destructive path,
- If my attitude needs to be put into check,
- If I need to hear the truth about a matter,

I prefer it be brought to my attention.

PROFOUND STATEMENT #1 - Once you have shared the truth with individuals, it is up to the RECIEVERS what they do with that truth. Don't beat up on yourself because the TRUTH you shared wasn't well received.

Our responsibility is to PLANT THE SEED OF TRUTH.

WHAT RESPONSES CAN YOU EXPECT WHEN YOU SHARE THE TRUTH?

- Some people will flat out DENY the truth.
- Some people will embrace the truth by expressing great remorse.

3

- Some people will accept only parts of the truth revealed to them.
- Some people will do some internal reflections and demonstrate changed behaviors.
- Some people may act worst as a result of the truth being shared because they are content with their present conditions or situations.

To acknowledge a truth also means the possibility of change.

PROFOUND STATEMENT #2 - INDIVIDUALS OFTEN RECRUIT "YES" PEOPLE in their lives. They only want people in their circles who will tell them what they want to hear and not necessarily what they need to hear!

WORDS OF WISDOM FOR THOSE WHO SHY AWAY FROM THE TRUTH:

You will never reach your fullest potential in life if you don't EMBRACE THE TRUTH ABOUT YOURSELF.

WORDS OF WISDOM TO THOSE WHO OPT TO SHARE THE TRUTH WITH OTHERS:

Don't be so quick to judge people if you don't see immediate changes after sharing the truth. You must realize that many behaviors displayed by individuals are **deeply ingrained** and have been **learned** and **practiced** throughout the course of their lives.

CHANGE IS A PROCESS!

If you approach a conversation in the right way, it at least opens the door for future conversations.

FIVE TIPS ON HOW TO SHARE THE TRUTH WITHOUT BEING OFFENSIVE.

1. ASK FOR PERMISSION TO SHARE CANDIDLY.
2. SHARE THE TRUTH WITHOUT JUDGMENT.
3. SHARE THE TRUTH WITH A SPIRIT OF LOVE.
4. SHARE THE TRUTH ONLY AFTER BEING PROMPTED BY THE HOLY SPIRIT.
5. SHARE THE TRUTH IN PRIVATE.

Somebody's future may be contingent upon our willingness to gently speak truth into their lives. Pray before you approach another person, but always be frank and honest with the individual. You may not be liked, but you will be well-respected for speaking the truth.

PERSONAL NOTES:

Chapter 2

PUT DOWN THAT PEN
(DON'T YOU SIGN ON THAT DOTTED LINE)

Proverbs 6:1-5

1) *My child, if you co-sign a loan for a friend or guarantee the debt of someone you hardly know-*
2) *If you have trapped yourself by your agreement and are caught by what you said,*
3) *Quick, get out of it if you possibly can! You have placed yourself at your friend's mercy. Now swallow your pride; go and beg to have your name erased.*
4) *Don't put it off! Do it now! Don't rest until you do!*
5) *Save yourself like a deer escaping from a hunter, like a bird fleeing from a net.*

Co-signing is a forbidden practice to be avoided at all cost if possible.

King Solomon shares his great wisdom with us and admonishes us about the dangers of putting our name on another person's debt.

> **PROFOUND STATEMENT #3 - The moment you cosign with another person, you sign away a PORTION OF YOUR FINANCIAL FREEDOM.**

One of the worst mistakes you can ever make is taking on the debt of another person that you can't even afford to fit within your STRETCHED BUDGET.

- Many of us have good hearts.

7

- Many of us have great intentions.
- Many of us hate to see other people we love suffering.
- Many of us can't stand to see other people in a financial bind.

However, the QUICKEST WAY TO GET BURNED is to co-sign for another person's financial responsibility.

My mother was a wise woman and she would always say, **"Money and friendship don't mix. The best way to terminate a friendship is to involve money in the equation."**

It is a fact of life - PEOPLE WILL BORROW FROM YOU and then get upset with you about your own money when you seek to retrieve it.

Whenever we co-sign for the debts of others, we become LEGALLY LIABLE.

- If they don't pay off the loan, it suddenly becomes our responsibility.
- If they fail to pay off the mortgage, we may end up paying for a home we can't live in.
- If they fail to pay off their car note, we may end up paying for a car we can't even drive.
- If they are late on their payments, it will impact our credit scores.

When the PRIMARY SIGNER fails to uphold the FINANCIAL OBLIGATION, the creditors will seek FINANCIAL RESTITUTION from the CO-SIGNER.

Unfortunately, some individuals have lost everything they have worked hard to acquire because they co-signed with their children, their siblings, friends, or significant others who ACTED FINANCIALLY IRRESPONSIBLY.

The SAD REALITY is other people usually don't care about how their lack of IRRESPONSIBILITY IMPACTS your future.

Some people don't mind **making contracts** and **breaking** them. Some people don't care about their bills getting behind because that's just a way of life for them.

My mother used to say, "**GOOD CREDIT IS SOMETIMES BETTER THAN HAVING CASH IN YOUR HAND.**" When your credit is good, it will speak for itself.

DON'T YOU SIGN YOUR FUTURE AWAY FOR ANYBODY! It is wise to avoid co-signing with people you know very well, but definitely don't co-sign with someone you barely know.

A MESSAGE TO YOUNG PEOPLE

DON'T GET YOURSELF TIED UP IN DEBT IN THE NAME OF LOVE. People will **enter** and **exit** your life continuously and they will leave you bearing a FINANCIAL BURDEN that will FINANCIALLY DEBILITATE YOU.

King Solomon urges us to run from a **co-signing obligation like a deer trying to escape from a hunter.** He urges us to run for our lives.

Secondly, King Solomon urges us to **flee from co-signing like a bird tries to flee from a net of entrapment.**

If you cannot help someone through a cash loan that will not hurt you if it is not returned, then don't put yourself in that predicament.

PROFOUND STATEMENT #4 - DON'T SIGN YOUR NAME ON THE DOTTED LINE OF ANYTHING AS A CO-SIGNER THAT YOU CAN'T AFFORD TO FINANCE IF THE OTHER PERSON'S INCOME WAS REMOVED FROM THE EQUATION.

FOUR REASONS WHY YOU SHOULD AVOID CO-SIGNING:

1) CO-SIGNING DESTROYS WHOLESOME FRIENDSHIPS AND RELATIONSHIPS.
2) CO-SIGNING PUTS YOU AT THE MERCY OF THE OTHER PERSON. You will always be walking around frantically worrying if they are going to fulfill their financial obligations.
3) CO-SIGNING WILL NEGATIVELY IMPACT YOUR CREDIT SCORE and PURCHASING POWER.
4) CO-SIGNING HINDERS YOUR ABILITY TO BE ABLE TO TAKE CARE OF YOUR OWN NEEDS.

Whatever you do, DON'T YOU SIGN ON THAT DOTTED LINE! RUN! IT'S A FINANCIAL TRAP! PUT DOWN THAT PEN!

PERSONAL NOTES:

Chapter 3

SELF-INFLICTED WOUNDS

Proverbs 29:18 *"When people do not accept divine guidance, they run wild. But whoever obeys the law is happy."*

MORAL RESTRAINT is a necessity in life. Listening to our **MORAL CONSCIENCE** is just as valuable. We often get upset with individuals for **INFLICTING** us with hurts and pains. However, many of our wounds are **SELF-INFLICTED**.

All believers receive **NOTIFICATION** through the **PERSON OF THE HOLY SPIRIT** when we are about to make a decision in life that is going to be devastating for us. We have the choice to **SHUN THE DEVASTATION** or to **IGNORE THE VOICE OF THE HOLY SPIRIT**.

Whenever we are given over to ourselves, we often make decisions that leave us spiritually broken.

PROFOUND STATEMENT #5 - YOU CAN BE YOUR OWN WORST ENEMY.

It is so easy to get entangled with the **cares**, **pleasures**, and **sinfulness** of this world and lose ourselves in the process. If we are not careful, each page of our **LIFE'S STORY** will be a **PAGE OF REGRETS**. Unfortunately, we can't go back and undo what has been done! King Solomon reminds us that God's Word is our guide for living. If we walk according to His Word, we can live a life **FULL OF HAPPINESS** and **JOY!**

Psalms 1:1 teaches us "Blessed is the man who does not follow the advice of the wicked, stand around with sinners, or join in with scoffers."

People often frown or shy away from the Word. Whenever our flesh wants to do something that is in rebellion against God's Word, we try to twist the Word to fit our situation.

King Solomon says whenever we ignore the Word of God, we simply find ourselves RUNNING WILD!

- We don't exercise moral restraint!
- We ignore our moral compasses or moral consciences!
- We close our ears to the truth!
- We cater to our flesh!
- We literally contribute to our own **SPIRITUAL DEMISE!**

The most difficult decision we will make in life is abstaining and walking away from stuff that our flesh is **BECKONING US TO PARTAKE IN!** Romans 1:24 declares - God will turn us over to our own reprobated minds when we continually ignore the voice of the Holy Spirit.

One of my sincerest prayers to the Lord is for Him to constantly deliver me from myself. It is my desire to please and to honor the Lord daily. Therefore, STARVING or CRUCIFYING my FLESH is a DAILY RITUAL.

FOUR THINGS WE CAN DO TO ENSURE THAT WE DON'T RUN WILD IN LIFE:

1) **SUBMIT DAILY TO THE WORD-** Stay in God's Word.
2) **SEEK GOD'S STRENGTH AND HELP-** Trust His strength. We cannot fight the temptation alone.

3) **SURRENDER OUR PASSION/WILLS TO GOD**. We must put our flesh to death daily and strive to do God's will.
4) **STRIVE TO LIVE A LIFE OF HOLINESS** and GODLINESS- Be ye holy because He is Holy.

PERSONAL NOTES:

Chapter 4

GIVE ME THE SOUP PLEASE

Proverbs 15:17- "A bowl of soup with someone you love is better than steak with someone you hate."

One of the greatest lessons we can teach our children in life is, "THEY WILL HAVE TO LEARN HOW TO CRAWL BEFORE THEY CAN WALK."

The second greatest lesson we can teach our children is, **"MONEY IS GREAT TO HAVE, BUT MONEY CANNOT BE A SUBSTITUTE FOR TRUE LOVE."**

We live in a FAST-PACED SOCIETY. Most people see something they desire and they convince themselves they must have it immediately. Even GOAL-DRIVEN PERSONS understand you cannot accomplish all of your goals and aspirations overnight.

Nothing weighs more heavily upon the hearts of parents than their children. People who don't have children are quick to say, "IF I HAD A CHILD, I WOULD NOT MAKE ALL THESE SACRIFICES." However, until they have children of their own, they don't know what they will or will not do. **Our children can bring us our greatest joys or they can be the source of our greatest sorrows in life.**

LOVING PARENTS DESIRE THE FOLLOWING FOR THEIR CHILDREN:

- They desire for their children to be safe.

- They desire for their children to establish a personal relationship with God.
- They desire for their children to be financially stable.
- They desire for their children to be healthy.
- They desire for their children to be wise.
- They desire for their children to excel in life.
- They desire for their children to be able to stand on their own two feet.
- They desire for their children to connect with wholesome people.
- They desire for their children to marry a suitable and caring spouse.

King Solomon speaks to this matter in Proverbs 15:17. He literally implies that we have to be careful who we allow into our PERSONAL SPACE

PROFOUND STATEMENT #6 - IT MAKES NO SENSE TO CATCH HELL OUTSIDE OF YOUR HOME ONLY TO RETURN HOME TO PUT UP WITH MORE HELL.

I have vowed the following:

- I am going to have peace in my home!
- I am going to relax in my home!
- I am going to find solitude and serenity within my home!

Home ought to be the escape from reality.
Home ought to be the place of retreat.

Home ought to be your safe haven.
Home ought to be your place of refreshment.

In this Season of your life you must recognize these PROFOUND REALITIES:

- Life is too short to spend it playing games!
- Life is too short to spend it in misery!
- Life is too short to spend it fighting and feuding!
- Life is too short to spend competing for your voice to be heard!
- Life is too short to spend all of your time trying to get someone else to value you.
- Life is too short to live it in fear on a daily basis!
- Life is too short to spend it being trampled upon!
- Life is too short to spend it being balled up in a fetal position because you are being mistreated.

YOU OWE YOURSELF BETTER OUT OF LIFE.

The kinds of relationships we establish will be important to our mental, emotional, spiritual, and physical well-being.

- We've got to be selective about who we allow into our private space!
- We've got to be careful about pouring our all into someone without getting to know that individual.
- We've got to be careful about becoming emotionally attached to a person until we have a full understanding of their thought processes.
- We can't afford to walk down the aisle and give our hand to someone in marriage without knowing what we are getting ourselves into.

It goes without saying, **IT TAKES TWO PEOPLE TO BUILD A WHOLESOME RELATIONSHIP.**

- Some people are unhappy because they have connected to the wrong person.
- Some people are unhappy because they have said "YES" to someone who does not have their INTEREST AT HEART!
- Some people are broken because the relationship they are in constantly drains them.
- Some people are miserable because their lifetime partner doesn't recognize their value and worth.

PROFOUND STATEMENT #7 - THE BEST STEP YOU CAN TAKE TO PREVENT SETTLING FOR MISERY IN A RELATIONSHIP IS SELF-LOVE. Love yourself because if you don't, nobody else will!

King Solomon encourages us to check out the **resume** of an individual before we give our hand to the person in marriage.

The CRITICAL QUESTION WE MUST ASK IS - "**WHAT'S IN YOUR HEART?**"

No matter how much you may love another person, if the individual doesn't possess a godly love for you, you will find yourself enduring a LIFETIME OF MISERY, PAIN, AND SUFFERING.

WHEN YOU CONNECT WITH THE RIGHT PERSON, THE FOLLOWING WILL HAPPEN:

- Your partner will bless you!
- Your partner will encourage you!
- Your partner will lavish you with unconditional love!
- Your partner will support you!

- Your partner will pray for you!
- Your partner will strengthen you!
- Your partner will push you towards your destiny!
- Your partner will pour into your life.

PROFOUND STATEMENT #8 - YOU CAN HAVE A MATCH MADE IN HEAVEN or BE CAUGHT UP IN A MATCH STRAIGHT FROM THE PIT OF HELL.

Some folk are miserable but they maintain a strong public image.

- In public, they appear to be the most loving couple.
- In public, they look as though they can eat each other up.
- In public, they look like the happiest couple on earth.
- In public, they communicate like they have it all together.

BEHIND CLOSED DOORS REALITY- THEY ARE LITERALLY LIVING OUT A NIGHTMARE! LIFE IS TOO PRECIOUS TO BE PUTTING ON A FRONT. IF THE RELATIONSHIP IS BROKEN, **GET SOME HELP!**

In Proverbs 15:17, King Solomon raises an interesting argument. He states a BOWL OF SOUP with someone you love is better than A STEAK with someone you hate.

PROFOUND STATEMENT #9 - A lot of the hurt and pain we encounter is often brought on by our own doing because we get so busy CHASING AFTER WHAT PEOPLE HAVE IN THEIR HANDS UNTIL WE FAIL TO EXAMINE WHAT'S IN THEIR HEARTS.

King Solomon simply encourages us to CHOOSE HAPPINESS over IMPRISONMENT.

We live in a materialistic society. When we enter into a relationship with the mindset of **GETTING ALL WE CAN** and **CANNING ALL WE GET**, WE SET OURSELVES UP TO BE MISHANDLED.

Although a person may be able to shower you with an ABUNDANCE OF MATERIAL GOODS, IF THE PERSON HAS A JACKED-UP HEART, YOU WILL NEVER BE COMPLETELY HAPPY.

- Money can't buy happiness.
- Stuff can't fulfill your spiritual needs.
- Stuff can't fulfill your emotional, mental, and physical needs.
- Stuff can't fill the void in your life.

PROFOUND STATEMENT #10 - IF YOU ARE ONLY WITH A PERSON BECAUSE OF THE STUFF THE INDIVIDUAL BRINGS TO THE TABLE, WHEN THE STUFF RUNS OUT, YOU HAVE ABSOLUTELY NOTHING!

IS THE PERSON YOU ARE THINKING ABOUT SPENDING THE REST OF YOUR LIFE WITH GOOD FOR YOU?

- Does the person degrade you?
- Does the person devalue you?
- Does the person recognize your value and your worth?
- Does the person pretend to love you in public, but abuses you behind closed doors?

WHAT KIND OF PERSON DO YOU NEED IN YOUR LIFE?

- You need a person in your life **who is going to be kind to you!**
- You need a person in your life **who is going to be compassionate towards you!**
- You need a person in your life **who is going to be forgiving towards you!**
- You need a person in your life **who is going to be patient with you!**
- You need a person in your life **who is going to be understanding of you!**
- You need a person in your life **who is going to be trustworthy.**
- You need a person in your life **who is willing to compromise!**
- You need a person in your life **who allows your voice to be heard!**
- You need a person in your life **who respects you!**
- You need a person in your life **who speaks life back into you.**

BEFORE YOU SETTLE FOR BEING WITH SOMEONE WHO DOES NOT LOVE YOU, YOU WILL BE BETTER OFF TAKING THE BOWL OF SOUP!

PAUSE - SOUP PLEASE!

- If you think you are going to run over me - SOUP PLEASE!
- If you think you are going to cuss at me - SOUP PLEASE!

- If you think I'm going to stick around while you drain me - SOUP PLEASE!
- If you think I'm going to allow you to abuse me - SOUP PLEASE!
- If you think I'm hanging around while you talk to me any kind of way - SOUP PLEASE!

YOU CAN HAVE THE HOUSE, THE TOYS, THE CAR, AND THE FIELD.

PROFOUND STATEMENT #11 - YOU WOULD BE BETTER OFF STARTING AT GROUND ZERO and WORK YOUR WAY BACK UP TO THE TOP RATHER THAN LIVE MISERABLE SIMPLY BECAUSE YOU ARE TRYING TO HOLD ON TO STUFF. LET IT GO!

SOME SIMPLE TRUTHS:
- You can get another house!
- You can get another car!
- You can build up another bank account!
- You can get another credit card!
- You can buy another steak!

HOWEVER, YOU MUST BE PROTECTIVE OF YOUR LIFE! YOU CAN REPLACE EVERYTHING EXCEPT YOURSELF.

5 WAYS YOU CAN DETERMINE WHAT IS IN THE HEART OF A PERSON

1. **LISTEN TO WHAT THE PERSON FOCUSES UPON-** Is the focus upon people or material things?

2. **LISTEN TO THE PERSON'S CONVERSATION ABOUT GOD** - Make sure you two are spiritually compatible.
3. **LISTEN TO THE PERSON'S VIEWS ABOUT TRYING TO HAVE SOMETHING OUT OF LIFE** - Is the person content or desires more out of life?
4. **LISTEN TO THE PERSON'S VIEWS ABOUT HOW YOU FIT INTO THE BIGGER PICTURE OF HIS OR HER LIFE** - Do you really have a place in the relationship?
5. **LISTEN TO THE PERSON'S VIEWS ABOUT FAMILY** - Is it all negativity? If so, beware of the signs!

FOUR LESSONS YOU NEED TO TAKE INTO EVERY RELATIONSHIP:

LESSON 1 - KNOW YOUR WORTH- You need to know your worth before you connect with somebody else or you will spend all of your life striving to be validated.

LESSON 2 - KNOW WHAT YOU EXPECT - Expect to be loved, nurtured, cared for, respected, supported, appreciated, and valued.

LESSON 3 - KNOW YOU ARE HOUSED WITH PURPOSE - Anybody who connects to you should be promoting your purpose and pushing you towards your destiny.

LESSON 4 - KNOW YOU SET THE STAGE FOR FUTURE GENERATIONS - Whatever you settle for, you are setting the stage for your sons and daughters. Make sure you set the stage right.

PERSONAL NOTES:

Chapter 5

APPRECIATE THE SMALL THINGS IN LIFE

Proverbs 27:7 - *"Honey seems tasteless to a person who is full, but even bitter food tastes sweet to the hungry."*

CRITICAL QUESTION- WHAT'S OUR MESSAGE TO THIS SPOILED GENERATION?

We are raising a GENERATION OF CHILDREN that has not been accustomed to struggling. We can't blame them because we have been their enablers. We have made sure they go LACKING FOR NOTHING.

What is the natural balance between **meeting their needs** and **teaching our children responsibility?** A fine line exists between those two concepts.

Our youngest daughter, Chelsea, calls it "ADULTING". She called us up in August 2019 and requested that we not pay anymore of her bills. She didn't want our assistance. She wanted to experience what it would be like to STAND ON HER OWN TWO FEET WITHOUT ANY FINANCIAL SUPPORT FROM HER PARENTS.

We have honored Chelsea's request and she has done an AMAZING JOB. Her philosophy is, **"I'M GOING TO HAVE TO TOTALLY PROVIDE FOR MYSELF ONE DAY SO IT MIGHT AS WELL BE NOW!"**

King Solomon writes this proverb to remind us of how **PROSPERITY** has a tendency to spoil us. We get to the place where we don't value the simple things in life because we are so accustomed to having anything we desire!

Famine and **hard times** have a way of humbling us. Oftentimes we don't even recognize how blessed we have been. However, if we ever get **DOWN TO NOTHING**, we learn to value the simple things in life.

My two daughters have been fortunate throughout the course of their lives. They have never really lacked for anything. All of their needs were SUFFICIENTLY PROVIDED!

My grandson, Landon, is such a joy. Admittedly, he is spoiled rotten by everyone who has a hand in his life. All of his needs have been BOUNTIFULLY PROVIDED. He is quick to say when he comes over to the house, **"Pops, I don't eat that"** or **"Pops, I don't do those kinds of cereals or that kind of sausage"**.

When I was growing up, you didn't have options. I simply ate whatever my mother was able to put on the table. My mother lived on a monthly public assisted income! She had to stretch those funds and make them last an entire month.

As I child, I was taught not to complain, but to be grateful because some children didn't have any food to eat.

The meals my mother prepared were not fancy, but they were filling.

- Sometimes the meal consisted of just a pot of black-eyed peas, neckbones, and a pan of cornbread.
- Sometimes the meal consisted of a pot of chicken backs and rice and a pan of cornbread.
- Sometimes the Sunday meal was fried chicken, cornbread, collard/turnip greens, and rice.

Nothing was wasted. **The leftovers were put up and we ate them along with whatever new meal was prepared the next day.**

Honestly, I didn't even realize how poor we were because I just assumed that everyone in the neighborhood ate like us.

Those humble beginnings prepared me for times of shortages and famines. Although, I don't ever want to return back to that kind of living, at least I know how to **SURVIVE BECAUSE OF IT!**

PROFOUND STATEMENT #12 - TEACHING OUR CHILDREN SELF-SUFFICIENCY IS AN ABSOLUTE REQUIREMENT IF WE WANT THEM TO SURVIVE.

One of the wisest men in the world, King Solomon declared - YOU DON'T KNOW HOW BLESSED YOU ARE UNTIL IT APPEARS THAT BLESSINGS HAVE SLIPPED AWAY FROM YOU.

- When you have an abundance, you will even frown up at a good steak.
- When you have an abundance, you tend to be more wasteful.
- When you have an abundance, it is hard to appreciate crumbs and leftovers.
- When you have an abundance, you don't focus on saving for a rainy day.

However, if you get down to nothing, you are no longer picky. HUNGER PAINS will teach you to eat the first thing set before you.

LIFE IS FULL OF SURPRISES!

- Since we don't know what the future holds,
- Since we don't know what kind of famine or shortage is coming,
- Since we don't know when our lot in life may change,

We better learn to live each day with a keener sense of appreciation.

King Solomon encourages us to **LEARN TO APPRECIATE THE SMALL** and **SIMPLE THINGS IN LIFE.**

My mother used to say to us - **"If someone gives you a slice of bread and offers you a cool drink of water, be grateful because people don't have to be nice."**

My mother also taught us - **"When someone gives you something, don't turn your nose up at or act ungrateful because sometimes you are blessed in order to be a blessing."**

King Solomon declares that **HUNGER PAINS WILL MAKE YOU EAT WHAT YOU SAY YOU WOULD NEVER TRY!**

4 LESSONS YOU NEED TO LEARN TO ENSURE YOU ALWAYS FOCUS UPON THE SMALL THINGS IN LIFE:

1) **REMEMBER THE SACRIFICES OTHERS MADE TO GET YOU WHERE YOU ARE TODAY.**
2) **REMEMBER YOU HAVE NO IDEA OF WHAT THE FUTURE HOLDS.**
3) **REMEMBER TO PREPARE FOR A RAINY DAY.**
4) **REMEMBER YOU ARE OFTEN BLESSED IN ORDER TO BE A BLESSING.**

PERSONAL NOTES:

Chapter 6

LIVE THE LIFE OF A GIVER

Proverbs 11:24 - *"It is possible to give freely and become more wealthy, but those who are stingy will lose everything."*

A song by the **CARAVANS entitled,** *YOU CAN'T BEAT GOD'S GIVING NO MATTER HOW YOU TRY,* are the lyrics ringing in my ears when I read this particular proverb.

The best way to **FREE YOURSELF FROM A LIFE OF GREED** is **TO LIVE TO BE A BLESSING!**

You will discover that the more you **POUR INTO OTHER PEOPLE**, the more the **LORD WILL POUR BACK INTO YOU**.

The Word of God teaches us to hold loosely the things of this world. Why? - Because properties and things are so transient.

- You could lose your house in a fire or storm.
- You could lose all of your investments during a stock market crash.
- Your car could be destroyed in an automobile accident.
- Everything you own could slide right out of the palm of your hand in a matter of seconds.

The Apostle Paul teaches us in Colossians 3:2 - "Set your affections and mind on the things above and not on the stuff of this world. In other words, he teaches us to BE GRATEFUL, but not GREEDY!

In Job 1:21, he stated "Naked I came from my mother's womb, and naked shall I return to thither..."

I Timothy 6:7 states, "For we brought nothing into this world and we can't take anything away."

LISTED BELOW ARE SOME REALITIES WE MUST FACE:

- All the stuff we work hard to acquire will be left for someone else's enjoyment and pleasure!
- All the furniture we have covered and will not sit on will fall into some less conscientious hands!
- All the China Dishes we are preserving for special occasions will either be broken dish by dish or auctioned off.

The thoughts we must take away from these realities are the following:

- Enjoy some of the fruits of your hard labor!
- Don't store up all your money and allow it to collect dust!
- Live Wholesomely!
- Live Wisely!
- Live Happily!
- Live Responsibly!

You only have one life to live so LIVE IT TO THE FULLEST.

Your **FIST IS LIKE A CONDUIT**! IT IS THE PIPELINE or CHANNEL through which everything flows. If you keep a **TIGHT FIST** and **BE STINGY**, you will not have a continuous flow coming into your life. However, if you open your fist allowing stuff to go out and to come in, your CUPBOARD WILL NEVER GO LACKING!

DON'T GET ALL YOU CAN and **CAN ALL YOU GET!** If you have been blessed, turn around and be a blessing.

One of the greatest fears we wrestle with is that of being manipulated and tricked by swindlers. The Holy Spirit will speak to you about your SHARING and POURING into others. Exercise your SPIRIT OF DISCERNMENT.

Whenever you are led by the Holy Spirit to bless somebody, BE OBEDIENT. God sees your faithfulness. You can never go wrong because your Heavenly Father owns the cattle upon a thousand hills (Psalm 50:10). He can supply all of your needs according to His riches in glory (Phil 4:19). Remember, God does not withhold any good things from us; therefore, He does not desire for us to go through life TIGHT-FISTED.

King Solomon teaches us - **When we give to others from the heart, it is possible for us to become wealthy, but those who are stingy will lose everything because they have nothing going out and nothing coming in.**

The Apostle Paul adds to the argument by decreeing in Ephesians 3:20 - "God can do exceedingly abundantly above all we can ask or think." WE WILL NEVER BE ABLE TO OUTGIVE GOD!

PERMIT ME TO SHARE FOUR REASONS WHY WE OUGHT TO GIVE.

1) **GIVING FREES US FROM GREED AND SELFISHNESS.**
2) **GIVING HONORS GOD.**
3) **GIVING SETS US UP TO BE BLESSED.**
4) **GIVING SPEAKS VOLUMES CONCERNING THE LOVE WE HAVE IN OUR HEARTS FOR OTHERS.**

LIVE THE LIFE OF A GIVER!

PERSONAL NOTES:

Chapter 7

POSSESS THE SPIRIT OF A GO-GETTER

Proverbs 12:27 - *"Lazy people don't even cook the game they catch, but the diligent make use of everything they find."*

Proverbs 13:4 - *"Lazy people want much, but get little, but those who work hard will prosper and be satisfied."*

The SPIRIT OF A GO-GETTER is becoming rare. Many people seem to want something for nothing.

GO-GETTERS are TRENDSETTERS! They don't waste all of their time talking, but they are PEOPLE OF ACTION. They ESTABLISH A PLAN and then WORK THE PLAN.

Unfortunately, we seem to be raising a GENERATION ENGULFED WITH THE MENTALITY THAT THEY ARE OWED SOMETHING!

I witness the WORK ETHICS OF PEOPLE EVERY SINGLE DAY and oftentimes those ethics are DEPLORABLE.

We must teach our children and grandchildren that nothing comes easy. IF THEY WANT BETTER OUT OF LIFE, THEY MUST PREPARE THEMSELVES TO COMPETE WITH THE BEST OF THE BEST.

- We are not just competing with ourselves.
- We are not just competing with other Americans.
- We are competing on a global level!
- We are competing with very sophisticated technology systems!

- We are competing with individuals whose work ethics are much more competitive.

King Solomon paints a very grim picture of LAZY PEOPLE! He says they are too sorry to lift a finger. They will actually go out and kill the wild life necessary for their survival, but upon returning home with the wild game, they become too lazy to clean it and cook it.

However, King Solomon contrasts the mindset of the lazy with those who are diligent. DILIGENT INDIVIDUALS HAVE A STRONG INNER DRIVE! They desire more out of life; therefore, they take advantage of EVERY OPPORTUNITY THAT IS SET BEFORE THEM.

PEOPLE HAVE A TENDANCY TO CRITICIZE GO-GETTERS

- GO-GETTERS are resourceful!
- GO-GETTERS believe where there is a will there is a way!
- GO-GETTERS don't give up at the first sign of trouble!
- GO-GETTERS want better for themselves and the generations to follow!
- GO-GETTERS look for opportunities in the midst of obstacles!
- GO-GETTERS expect to TRIUMPH ABOVE TRIALS!
- GO-GETTERS are not afraid to make STRATEGIC MOVES!
- GO-GETTERS are constantly working behind the scenes to PRODUCE!
- GO-GETTERS tend to be TRENDSETTERS and TRAILBLAZERS!

King Solomon says **LAZY PEOPLE** are just **WISHFUL THINKERS**! They don't have any real intentions of doing anything about their current state. They are merely **DAYDREAMERS**. They are content with life as it is at the moment. Years down the road, they will still be singing their WISHFUL TUNES!

Productive diligent individuals will work from sunrise to sunset to get their work completed. They are GOAL-ORIENTED.

- They understand the value of SEIZING THE MOMENT!
- They understand the IMPORTANCE OF TAKING ADVANTAGE OF EVERY OPPORTUNITY SET BEFORE THEM.
- They equate **wasted times** to **wasted dreams.**
- They don't render EXCUSES, they yield RESULTS!

LAZY PEOPLE SEEK OUT SOMEBODY TO BLAME FOR THEIR FAILURES IN LIFE.

GO-GETTERS SEEK AN OPEN DOOR OR A CHANCE TO PROVE THEMSELVES.

4 STEPS ARE NECESSARY TO ACHIEVE SUCCESS IN LIFE

1) **YOU MUST PUT CHRIST FIRST!**
2) **YOU MUST PRIORITIZE!**
3) **YOU MUST PERSEVERE!**
4) **YOU MUST PURSUE YOUR DESTINY AT ALL COST**

GET UP OFF YOUR BEHIND AND GET MOVING!

DESTINY IS CALLING!

YOU DON'T HAVE ANOTHER MOMENT TO WASTE!

PERSONAL NOTES:

Chapter 8

BEWARE OF THE GOSSIPER

Proverbs 20:19 - *"A gossip tells secrets, so don't hang around someone who talks too much."*

> **PROFOUND STATEMENT #13 - DON'T LET YOUR SECRET JEWELS FALL INTO THE WRONG HANDS.**

My constant prayer to the Lord is, "DELIVER ME FROM THE PATHWAY OF GOSSIPERS". I don't desire to be in the PATHWAY OF ANYONE WHO HAS A HURTFUL TONGUE!

Because I am vibrant and full of life, I host a certain circle that brings me joy!

- I enjoy people who like to laugh.
- I enjoy people who are full of life.
- I enjoy people who have good things to say about others.
- I enjoy people who are always praying for others.
- I enjoy people who are constantly building others!
- I enjoy people who are compassionate towards others.

I RUN FROM PEOPLE WHO ALWAYS SEEM TO HAVE THEIR MOUTHS ON OTHER PEOPLE.

The words flowing from the mouth of King Solomon are POWERFUL! He really says **A GOSSIPER CAN'T BE TRUSTED!**

My mother used to say, "**DON'T ALLOW PEOPLE TO MAKE A TRASH CAN OUT OF YOU OR ELSE THEY WILL ALWAYS BE DUMPING STUFF ON YOU!**"

My mother also used to say, "**BE CAREFUL WHO BRINGS YOU A BONE ABOUT OTHER PEOPLE BECAUSE THEY WILL CARRY A BONE ABOUT YOU!**" Simply stated, if they will talk about other people, they will also talk about you.

My mindset is the following:

- If you are not saying something good about other people,
- If you are not saying something to empower other people,
- If you are not going to strive to restore other people,
- If you are not going to pray other people through what they are dealing with,

YOU SHOULD REMAIN SILENT!

WHENEVER I CROSS THE PATH OF A GOSSIPER, I EXERCISE TWO COURSES OF ACTION.

First, I try to REDIRECT THE CONVERSATION OF THE GOSSIPER TOWARDS SOMETHING POSITIVE.

Secondly, if I am UNSUCCESSFUL AT REDIRECTING THE CONVERSATION, MY B-PLAN is to ALTER MY PATH!

I ABSOLUTELY REFUSE TO GET ENTANGLED WITH THE GOSSIPER!

WE MUST UNDERSTAND THE FOLLOWING:

- Gossip can be poisonous.
- Gossip can unfairly bias our opinions and view about other people.

41

- Gossip can cause us to cast unfair judgment upon people.
- Gossip can taint and tarnish the reputation of innocent people.
- Gossip can leave people scarred.

Have you ever been burned by gossip?

Have you ever had to defend your reputation or image against gossip?

PROFOUND STATEMENT #14 - BEWARE OF PEOPLE WHO ALWAYS HAVE SOMETHING NEGATIVE TO TELL YOU ABOUT EVERYBODY EXCEPT YOU! WHEN THE OPPORTUNITY ARISES, YOU WILL BE THEIR NEXT TARGET!

UTILIZE THE FOUR SECRETS BELOW TO DEFEND AGAINST THE GOSSIP SPOKEN CONCERNING YOU:

1) NEVER CHASE BEHIND THE UNTRUES OF LIFE.
2) NEVER ALLOW GOSSIP TO DERAIL YOUR PURPOSE (Don't lose sight of your assignment or purpose).
3) NEVER FEEL OBLIGATED TO ANSWER TO THE LIES OF A GOSSIPER.
4) NEVER ALLOW A GOSSIPER SEE YOU SWEAT.

DEAL WITH YOUR HURT, SCARS, PAINS, and BROKENNESS BEHIND CLOSED DOORS. Never give gossipers the pleasure of knowing they have broken you. If so, they will seek to DIG DEEPER INTO YOUR WOUNDS!

If you have been the VICTIM OF MALICIOUS GOSSIP, remember you are not who they say you are!

If you HOLD YOUR HEAD HIGH, YOU WILL RISE ABOVE THE LIES!

A lie will take off like a WILDFIRE, but if you DON'T ADD FUEL TO THE FIRE. IT WILL SOON BURN OFF.

PERSONAL NOTES:

Chapter 9

QUARREL BY YOURSELF
(WASTED ENERGY AND BREATH)

Proverbs 17:14 - *"Beginning a quarrel is like opening a floodgate, so drop the matter before a dispute breaks out."*

THE POWER OF EFFECTIVE COMMUNICATION is devalued in most relationships.

After being in ministry for more than 37 years, I have discovered that people **TALK AT EACH OTHER all the time**, but they **DON'T TALK TO EACH OTHER ENOUGH**. Most conversations go haywire when individuals allow QUARRELING TO DOMINATE THE TALK SESSION.

King Solomon takes a moment to address the **SENSELESSNESS OF USING NEGATIVE WORDS TO ENGAGE IN VERBAL FIGHTING!**

You have heard the cliché, "MISERY LOVES COMPANY". Oftentimes you will cross the paths of people whose primary objective is to PICK ARGUMENTS WITH OTHER PEOPLE!

Unfortunately, some people live to argue. They literally get a thrill out of quarrelling. Most of us are DRAWN INTO THEIR QUARRELSOME WEBS without even recognizing what has happened to us.

Former First Lady of the United States, Michelle Obama stated, **"Our family's motto is WHEN THEY GO LOW, WE GO HIGH!"**

We cannot afford to allow people to draw us into the SAD WORLD OF QUARRELING!

LISTED BELOW ARE SOME REALITIES WE MUST ACCEPT:

- We can't fix other people, but we can strive to become better ourselves.
- We can't control what comes out of the mouths of other people, but we can pray to the Lord to bridle our tongues.
- We are not responsible for how people treat us, but we are accountable for how we treat them.
- We must learn that walking away from a senseless argument doesn't make us a coward, but it demonstrates who is the bigger person.

USUALLY THERE ARE THREE SIDES TO EVERY ARGUMENT:

- YOUR SIDE
- THEIR SIDE
- TRUE SIDE

Most of us are going to promote **our side** whether that be the reality or not.

King Solomon argues that when the FLOODGATES TO OUR MOUTHS ARE OPEN, THINGS BEGIN TO SPIN OUT OF CONTROL REAL FAST.

Once words have been **RELEASED** into the atmosphere, we cannot **RETRIEVE** them back. Therefore, we must recognize that what we speak can **HAVE A LASTING IMPRESSION UPON OTHERS long after the argument has subsided.**

THE PURPOSE OF FLOODGATES

- Floodgates are designed to restrain or to contain certain items.
- Floodgates are designed to hold back things that could wreak havoc in the world.
- Floodgates are designed to keep things in check.

If there is a BREECH TO A FLOODGATE, STUFF STARTS OVERFLOWING AND DESTROYIING EVERYING WITHIN ITS PATHS.

God has blessed us with TWO FLOODGATES. Our **upper** and **bottom** lips are designed to RESTRAIN OUR TONGUE. Once the floodgates are opened, if we are not guided by the Holy Spirit and His Word, we can do some major damage with our mouth.

- Friendships are destroyed by loose tongues.
- Marriages are destroyed by poisonous tongues.
- Families are destroyed by loose lips.
- Business deals go sour because of unrestrained tongues.

What is the benefit of a nasty and heated verbal fight?

What is really accomplished when two people start lashing out at each other?

Who is the winner/loser in an UNWHOLESOME ARGUMENT? If truth be told, NOBODY WINS!

Most arguments DO MORE DAMAGE THAN GOOD! Years of hard work in a marriage, relationship, or friendship can go down the drain quickly if individuals involved DON'T RESTRAIN THEIR TONGUES.

JUST BECAUSE YOU THINK IT, DOESN'T MEAN YOU HAVE TO SPEAK IT. We are quick to say, "I Just speak my mind."

WHY DO PEOPLE ARGUE (FROM A POSITIVE PERSPECTIVE)?

- People argue because they desire to be heard.
- People argue because they feel the need to be acknowledged.
- People argue because they need to get something off their chest.
- People argue because they feel their views are not being respected.
- People argue because they are often crying out for help or attention.

WHY DO PEOPLE ARGUE (FROM A NEGATIVE PERSPECTIVE)?

- People argue when they have unresolved issues within themselves so they often lash out at others.
- People argue because they are controlling.
- People argue because they feel they must have the last word.
- People argue because they have not been taught a better way to communicate.
- People argue out of pure meanness of heart.
- People argue because they are verbal bullies.

King Solomon advises us to refrain from QUARRELING BECAUSE IT OFTEN LEADS TO OTHER FORMS OF UGLINESS. A quarrel may start out small and with a simple exchange of words; however, the more heated the conversation becomes, the argument becomes problematic for everyone involved.

- Arguing leads to raised voices.
- Arguing leads to harsh name calling.
- Arguing leads to the hashing out of old and buried issues.
- Arguing leads to a major breakdown of communication.
- Arguing leads to regrettable words being spoken.
- Arguing leads to physical confrontations.
- Arguing leads to destruction of wholesome relationships.

SOME FOLK DON'T THINK TWICE ABOUT QUARRELING BECAUSE...

- They enjoy hurting other people.
- They feel empowered when they argue.
- They thrive off of injuring others with their words.
- They enjoy making other people feel small and belittled.
- They use arguments to create fear in others.
- They use arguments to imprison other people mentally, emotionally, physically, and psychologically.

I TEACH MY DAUGHTERS TO AVOID HEATED ARGUMENTS AT ALL COSTS IF IT IS POSSIBLE.

I ALSO TEACH MY GIRLS THAT IF A MAN WILL YELL AND SCREAM AT YOU, HE WILL ABUSE YOU. IF HE WILL ABUSE YOU, HE WILL ALSO KILL YOU IN A MOMENT OF RAGE.

Deborah and I share almost 35 years of marriage and dating. We made certain vows to each other that have been paramount in keeping our marriage solid.

- We vowed never to bash each other with harsh words!
- We vowed never to allow an argument to blind us of our love for each other.
- We vowed not to let the sun go down on our wrath or to go to bed angry with each other.
- We vowed to AGREE TO DISAGREE and to leave some matters of discussions for a later date until we could discuss them calmly, rationally, and respectfully.

Those principles have to be practiced within every relationship within your life.

- ARGUMENTS can lead to RESENTMENT
- RESENTMENT can lead to BITTERNESS.
- BITTERNESS can lead to HATRED.

HATRED can lead to utter DESTRUCTION.

PROFOUND STATEMENT #15 - YOU HAVE TOO MUCH HOUSED IN YOU TO STOOP TO THE LEVEL OF THE PERSONS WHO ARE ATTACKING YOU!

- Get your temper under control.
- Get your words under control.
- Get your mind sober.
- Get your emotions under control.

> **PROFOUND STATEMENT #16 - DON'T BECOME THE SPITTING IMAGE OF THE BEAST YOU DESPISE**

- Maintain your integrity at all costs.
- Maintain your spiritual composure.
- Maintain your Christian Witness.

DON'T BECOME A PREY TO A FLUNKY

Some folk already know they are not headed anywhere so they are being used by Satan to come after YOUR PURPOSE!

> **PROFOUND STATEMENT #17 - YOU ONLY HAVE SO MANY HOURS WITHIN A DAY. YOU GET TO CHOOSE WHO AND WHAT YOU WILL ALLOW TO TAKE UP THE TIMESLOTS WITHIN YOUR DAY. DON'T WASTE YOUR DAY AWAY ARGUING WITH FOLK OVER PETTY STUFF.**

MY PERSONAL PHILOSOPHY IS:

- If it doesn't impact my relationship with God,
- If it doesn't impact my relationship with Deborah and my girls,
- If it doesn't impact my livelihood,

I AM NOT GIVING YOU THE TIME OF DAY TO BE ENTERTAINED BY AN ARGUMENT WITH YOU!

LISTED BELOW ARE EIGHT TIPS ON HOW TO ARGUE WHOLESOMELY AND CLEAN!

1) ESTABLISH SOME NORMS FOR HAVING DISCUSSIONS. Agree that if a discussion starts going south, all parties will end it immediately.
2) ALLOW OTHERS TO SPEAK WITHOUT INTERRUPTIONS OR WITHOUT PRECONCEIVED JUDGMENTS. Don't come to the table loaded. Don't talk at each other, but talk to each other in love.
3) LISTEN ATTENTIVELY!
4) ACKNOWLEDGE WHEN YOU ARE WRONG!
5) SWALLOW YOUR PRIDE.
6) ASK FOR FORGIVENESS.
7) KEEP IN MIND WHAT'S IMPORTANT – THE RELATIONSHIP.
8) MOVE BEYOND THE ARGUMENT - Put it to rest. Let it go!

Proverbs 17:27 reads - *"A truly wise person uses few words: a person with understanding is even-tempered."*

THE POWER OF EFFECTIVE COMMUNICATION IS THE KEY TO SUSTAINING LONG TERM RELATIONSHIPS.

WHEN THE COMMUNICATION GOES, SO GOES THE RELATIONSHIP.

PERSONAL NOTES:

Chapter 10

ENGAGE IN DAILY LAUGHTER

Proverbs 17:22 - *"A cheerful heart is good medicine, but a broken spirit saps a person's strength."*

My personal charge to you is - **MAKE IT A RITUAL TO LAUGH EVERY DAY OF YOUR LIFE.**

LAUGHTER HAS TO BECOME A PRIORITY! Whatever you do, don't allow PEOPLE, PROBLEMS, PLIGHTS, AND PREDICAMENTS **ROB YOU OF YOUR ABILTIY TO LAUGH!**

LAUGHTER IS GOD'S DIVINE RELEASE VALVE IN YOUR LIFE!

LAUGHTER WILL HELP KEEP YOU SANE.

Growing up as a child, I would practically laugh about everything and anybody. Many of you grew up and your parents would say - **"TURN OFF YOUR GIGGLE/TICKLE BOXES"** or they would say, **"You just keep laughing at folk. One day it is going to catch up with you."** I didn't recognize what that meant as a child, but I understand it clearly now.

In life, we are to laugh with people and not at them.

By way of personal confession, I did not recognize the THERAPEUTIC POWER OF LAUGHTER. Laughter takes the EDGE OFF OF LIVING! Unfortunately, my TICKLE BOX will get turned on anywhere about the simplest things in life. Sometimes I laugh uncontrollably.

PROFOUND STATEMENT #18 - WHEN YOU STOP LAUGHING YOU LITERALLY STOP LIVING!

King Solomon declared, "LAUGHTER IS LIKE A NECESSARY MEDICATION. You need to take A DOSE DAILY."

When we observe the world around us,

- People are sad.
- People are broken.
- People are uptight.
- Peoples' nerves are on edge.
- People are almost at their breaking point.

IF THEY DON'T LAUGH, THEY ARE GOING TO COLLAPSE.

- They have to learn to laugh through the pain!
- They have to learn to laugh through the frustration.
- They have to laugh in the midst of the despondency.
- They have to laugh in spite of the despair!
- They have to laugh through the tears!
- They have to force themselves to laugh through the depression!

LAUGHTER WILL BREAK SO MANY YOKES!

LAUGHTER WILL BREAK SO MANY STRONGHOLDS!

LAUGHTER WILL CURE SO MANY AILMENTS!

We must understand the following:

- It's not God's will for us to walk around with our heads hung down in sorrow!

- It's not God's will for us to be full of sadness!
- It's not God's will for us to walk around emotionally broken!
- It's not God's will for us to live in despair and dismay.

The writer of Proverbs declares:

- When our spirits are broken, years are taken off of our lives.
- When our spirits are broken, we show our age quicker than expected.
- When our spirits are broken, we are robbed of our internal peace!
- When our spirits are broken, it hinders our ability to be our best!
- When our spirits are broken, it interferes with our productivity.

However, the writer of proverbs also declares:

- When our hearts are cheerful, we add years to our lives.
- When our hearts are cheerful, we bless others around us!
- When our hearts are cheerful, it changes the outcome of our day!
- When our hearts are cheerful, it strengthens our CHRISTIAN TESTIMONY.

Jesus came that we might have life and have it more abundantly (John 10:10). He came that our joy might be full and complete.

My admonition to us is -MAKE TIME FOR A DAILY LAUGH.

- We all have issues!
- We all have problems we are working through.

- We all have distractions pulling at our attention.
- We all have to face trying circumstances.

However, we owe it to ourselves **TO MUSTER UP ENOUGH ENERGY TO LAUGH.**

Many will be offended by your laugh, but laugh even harder. If they only knew your testimony and your personal story, they would join you in your laughter!

People often ask me, "What are you laughing about? They often follow up their question with the comment of, "I DON'T SEE ANYTHING FUNNY OR ANYTHING TO LAUGH ABOUT."

SADLY STATED—**THOSE INDIVIDUALS HAVE ALLOWED LIFE TO SUFFOCATE THEIR LAUGHTER!**

I have quickly learned I have two options in life.

Option A - I can laugh

Option B- I can cry

I CHOOSE TO LAUGH!

PERMIT ME TO END THIS CHAPTER BY GIVING YOU FIVE REASONS WHY YOU OUGHT TO LAUGH!

1) **LAUGH BECAUSE YOU ARE ALIVE!**
2) **LAUGH BECAUSE IT PROVIDES HEALING TO YOU!**
3) **LAUGH BECAUSE IT'S MEDICINE FOR OTHERS AROUND YOU!**
4) **LAUGH BECAUSE YOU HAVE SURVIVED WHAT KILLED OTHERS!**
5) **LAUGH BECAUSE IN HIM YOUR JOY IS COMPLETE!**

THE WORLD NEEDS LAUGHTER MORE THAN IT HAS EVER NEEDED IT BEFORE! YOU HAVE THE POWER TO START THE PARTY. Celebrate because breakthroughs and miracles are going to come through your laughter! PRAISE THE LORD!

PERSONAL NOTES:

Chapter 11

MODEL KINDNESS

Proverbs 11:17 - *"Your own soul is nourished when you are kind, but you destroy yourself when you are cruel."*

Some people are **DAILY PRACTITIONERS OF CRUELTY.**

It takes a lot of energy to BE CRUEL. It requires little or no effort to BE KIND! CRUELTY DAMAGES YOU PHYSICALLY, EMOTIONALLY, SPIRITUALLY, and MENTALLY!

The writer of Proverbs teaches us - **YOU MAY THINK YOU ARE HURTING OTHERS BY BEING CRUEL, BUT THE GREATEST DAMAGE IS BEING DONE TO YOURSELF.**

However, kindness adds VALUE to your life. You can experience no greater personal gratification than that of knowing you have PERFORMED PERSONAL ACTS OF KINDNESS TOWARDS OTHERS.

Happy people are usually kind people. Miserable and unhappy people are usually cruel in nature. Each of us gets to choose what kind of person we will be!

DON'T ALLOW THE ACTIONS, NEGATIVITY, AND BITTER RESPONSE OF OTHER PEOPLE CAUSE YOU TO RESPOND WITH BITTERNESS.

It is not the major acts of kindness that we perform that usually bring joy to our lives, but simple acts such as:

- Being supportive
- Giving a hug
- Sharing an encouraging word
- Leaving someone a positive note
- Giving someone an uplifting phone call
- Greeting people with a warm smile

ALL THESE SIMPLE ACTS MAKE A MAJOR DIFFERENCE.

The world is reeking with **BITTERNESS** and **HATRED.** Let's do our part by simply BEING KIND!

- When we are kind, we reveal what's in our hearts!
- When we are kind, we give strength to others!
- When we are kind, we represent Christ's AMAZING LOVE!
- When we are kind, we add a different flavor to the earth.

Being CRUEL, MEAN, INCONSIDERATE, SELFISH, HATEFUL, SPITEFUL, and BITTER towards others is not a REFLECTION OF GOD!

Some people THRIVE ON NEGATIVE ENERGY and when you become NEGATIVE, **YOU BECOME TOXIC TO EVERTHING** and **EVERYONE IN YOUR PATH.**

If you are not careful, you could pass that NEGATIVE ENERGY on to your children and grandchildren. The toxicity will end up destroying every relationship you engage in.

King Solomon declares - When we are kind, we nurture our souls, but when we are cruel, we destroy ourselves.

I need my soul NOURISHED!

I need my soul FED!

I need my soul SUSTAINED!

I need my soul ENCOURAGED!

PROFOUND STATEMENT #19 - Don't give people control of your emotional tank. You stay in control of you!

Listed below are 4 COMMON PRACTICES THAT WILL HELPS US WITH KINDNESS:

1) THINK BEFORE YOU ACT!
2) TASTE YOUR WORDS BEFORE YOU DISH THEM OUT!
3) TREAT OTHERS AS YOU DESIRE TO BE TREATED!
4) STRIVE TO PLEASE GOD IN ALL OF YOUR ACTIONS!

Perform one act of kindness daily and eventually it will become HABITUAL within your life.

PERSONAL NOTES:

Chapter 12

LISTEN TO SOMEBODY

Proverbs 29:1 - *"Whoever stubbornly refuses to accept criticism will suddenly be broken beyond repair."*

> **PROFOUND STATEMENT #20 - WE ALL POSSESS A RELUCTANT SPIRIT WHEN IT COMES DOWN TO ACCEPTING NEGATIVITY. HOWEVER, IT IS ESSENTIAL TO EMBRACE CONSTRUCTIVE CRITICISM.**

In this proverb, King Solomon really chimes in on the DANGER OF NOT HEEDING SOUND ADVICE.

Life is full of people who focus on nothing but negativity. They pride themselves on being negative. They are PROFESSIONAL CRITICIZERS! They find fault in everybody and everything. They are literally the type of people you RUN from when you see them headed in your direction. None of us should listen to the CONSTANT DESTRUCTIVE CRITICISM of other people and then allow that NEGATIVITY TO DEFINE US.

However, we must learn how to EXERCISE A WHOLESOME SPIRIT OF DISCERNMENT! Godly discernment will help us to distinguish between DESTRUCTIVE and CONSTRUCTIVE CRITICISM.

- The Lord has placed certain people in our lives to help us maintain wholesome perspectives.

- The Lord has purposefully placed people in our paths to serve as honest accountability partners.
- The Lord has surrounded us with a host of strong personalities who are not afraid to call us on the carpet when they see we are stepping out of line.

PROFOUND STATEMENT #21 - ALL OF OUR INTENTIONS MAY BE GOOD, BUT THAT DOESN'T MEAN THAT EVERY DECISION WE MAKE IN LIFE IS FLAWLESS!

WE ALL NEED **SPIRITUAL SOUNDING BOARDS** WITHIN OUR LIVES. It is paramount for us to have a group of level-headed people to serve as **FILTER CHECKERS** for our ideas. Without spiritual sounding boards, the following dangers exist:

- We will go through life believing that our way of thinking is the **BEST** or **ONLY WAY**.
- We will go through life **DISMISSING** everything others bring to our attention.
- We will go through life with a **PRIDEFUL ATTITUDE**.
- We will go through life in **SECLUSION** thus failing to recognize and embrace all the other great ideas surrounding us.

PROFOUND STATEMENT #22 – THE WORST MISTAKE WE CAN EVER MAKE IS TO DEVALUE A PERSON WHO IS TELLING US SOMETHING FOR OUR OWN BENEFIT!

King Solomon argues when we become so stubborn that we refuse to listen to anybody, we become broken beyond repair. He argues there is NO HOPE FOR PEOPLE WHO STICK THEIR FINGERS IN THER EARS and IGNORE SOUND ADVICE.

When you are the CONSTRUCTIVE CRITICIZER and your advice is not welcomed, sometime you have to STEP BACK and ALLOW STUBBORN PEOPLE TO HIT ROCK BOTTOM. You cannot POUR GOOD INFORMATION INTO THE LIFE OF SOMEONE WHO IS NOT OPEN TO IT.

As a child growing up, I didn't understand this cliché shared by my mother. She would say, "IF YOU MAKE YOUR BED HARD, YOU ARE GOING TO HAVE TO LAY IN IT". The older I got, the more I understood the underlying message embedded within that saying.

Simply stated, my mother was trying to teach me that every action has a set of consequences. She was also trying to teach that each person is responsible for the consequences heaped upon his or her life.

SOUND ADVICE PROVIDED TO PERSONS ASPIRING TO BLOSSOM IN LIFE

- Don't push away people who hold you accountable.
- Don't push away people who are vested in you!
- Don't push away the people who are the greatest promoters of your destiny.
- Don't push away the people who are encouraging you to dream big.
- Don't push away the people who are trying to teach you how to have something in life.

THREE VALUABLE LESSONS WE UNDERSTAND ABOUT CONSTRUCTIVE CRITICISM

1) CONSTRUCTIVE CRITICISM IS ALWAYS GIVEN WITH THE HOPE OF BRINGING ABOUT RESTORATION AND HEALING!
2) CONSTRUCTIVE CRITICISM IS OF NO VALUE UNLESS IT IS FULLY EMBRACED BY THE RECEIVER.
3) CONSTRUCTIVE CRITICISM CAN BE THE GAMECHANGER WHEN IT IS SHARED IN LOVE.

PERSONAL NOTES:

Chapter 13

OWN IT-UNCOVER IT

Proverbs 28:13 - *"People who cover over their sins will not prosper. But if they confess and forsake them, they will receive mercy."*

The first step to **RECOVERY** is admitting we have a problem.

SELF-ADMISSION is tough for most of us. Other people can bring issues to our attention such as drinking, gambling, pornography, gluttony, greed, pride, hatefulness, anger, etc. but if we cannot admit the PROBLEM to ourselves, we will never SEEK HELP!

Most of us believe we can fix our own issues. We are too prideful to acknowledge we are in OVER OUR HEADS. Therefore, we SINK or almost DROWN before we cry out for help. Even when we are sinking, many times pride will not allow us to REACH OUT FOR HELP! Oftentimes, even when we know we are WRONG, we would rather COVER UP OUR DIRT rather than ACKNOWLEDGE OUR FLAWS.

SOME REALITIES WE MUST ACCEPT

- All of us have sinned.
- All of us have done some stuff we regret in life.
- All of us wish we could turn back the hands of time and do some things differently.
- All of us have room for improvement!
- All of us have imperfections within our lives.
- All of us are in need of God's mercy and grace.

We ought to be striving to walk, talk, act, live, and shine like Jesus daily; however, sometimes we fall short.

> **PROFOUND STATEMENT #23 - OUR ISSUE IS NOT IN OUR GREATEST SHORTFALL! THE REAL ISSUE RESIDES IN OUR STUBBORNNESS OR UNWILLINGNESS TO GET ON OUR FACES BEFORE GOD.**

We may feel the need to PUT ON A FRONT for everyone else within our lives, but we can keep it real with the Lord.

- He already knows we are flawed.
- He already knows we have some spiritual proclivities.
- He knows we battle with some private stuff we are too ashamed to talk to others about.
- He already knows the REAL PERSON BEHIND THE MASK.

Therefore, covering up our sins or issues only make matters worse.

- Covering up our sin can lead to further deception.
- Covering up our flaws and issues can lead to a greater degree of comfortability.
- Covering up our mess can lead to us feeling utterly defeated.
- Covering up our sins can cause us to try to justify them.
- Covering up our sins can hinder us from receiving the help we need.
- Covering up our sins can leave us feeling weighted down.

- Covering up our sins can permanently IMPRISON US SPIRITUALLY.

Because I desire to live a FREE and WHOLESOME LIFE, COVERING UP SIN IS NOT AN OPTION FOR ME! I have to make daily confessions and plead with the Lord for strength.

King Solomon urges us to get rid of the weight of sin by doing two things.

First, he admonishes us to **CONFESS** our sins.

- We have to acknowledge we are broken.
- We have to acknowledge we are helpless.
- We have to acknowledge we are in need of Divine Power.

Second, he admonishes us to **FORSAKE** our sins. Confession alone is not sufficient. Admission of guilt is only the first step. Admission of guilt opens the doorway for conversation with God. Forsaking our sins involves so much more.

- Forsaking sins involves repentance.
- Forsaking sins involves a mindset change.
- Forsaking sins involves a change of heart.
- Forsaking sins involves a change of behavior.

To CONFESS OUR SINS, but then continue to WALLOW IN THEM is a SLAP IN THE FACE TO GOD.

King Solomon reminds us that God is waiting to assist those who are struggling. The Lord is waiting to assist those who are sincere about their plight in life. The Lord is waiting to assist those who want to experience a wonderful change only He can bring about within their lives. King Solomon argues:

- God will show us mercy!
- God will show us patience!
- God will assist us with our healing!
- God will withhold the penalty we rightfully deserve.
- God will provide us with the counseling and therapy we need to make A FULL RECOVERY!

FOUR STEPS MUST OCCUR IF WE PLAN TO GET ON WITH THE REST OF OUR LIVES.

1) WE MUST CONFESS OUR SINS.
2) WE MUST SURRENDER OUR WILLS TO HIM.
3) WE MUST RELY UPON HIS STRENGTH FOR HEALING AND DELIVERANCE.
4) WE MUST PURPOSEFULLY LIVE FOR HIM.

PERSONAL NOTES:

Chapter 14

CONTROL YOUR TEMPER

Proverbs 29:22 - *"A hot-tempered person starts fights and gets into all kinds of sin."*

Unfortunately, we seem to be raising a very angry generation. I have witnessed this throughout the course of my career as an educator and during my tenure as a pastor.

For no apparent reason, people just seem to be angry. Even when you offer a kind hello and greet people with a warm smile, they are quick to say, "WHAT ARE YOU SMILING ABOUT", or "DON'T SAY GOOD MORNING TO ME BECAUSE THERE IS NOTHING GOOD ABOUT THIS DAY."

It is a given...

- All of us have bad days!
- All of us have a tendency to wake up on the wrong side of the bed!
- All of us have moments when we are not able to PUT ON OUR HAPPY FACE!
- All of us have days when our TEMPERS flare up.
- All of us have days when our TOLERANCE LEVELS are low!
- All of us have days when stuff on the job sets us off!
- All of us have times when things within our homes aggravate us.
- All of us have moments when issues within our friendship circles frustrate us.

HOWEVER, NONE OF THESE BEHAVIORS CAN BECOME OUR DAILY NORMS.

King Solomon argues, a hot-tempered person is a danger to him or herself. He argues that hot-tempered persons love to engage in petty fights.

Most of us have some acquaintances with MR. and MRS. HOT-HEAD. These individuals don't usually CONVERSATE RATIONALLY. They just GO OFF at the drop of a HAT! If one button is pushed within their lives, they are ready to fight.

PROFOUND STATEMENT #24 - HOT-TEMPERED PEOPLE USUALLY SELF-SABOTAGE.

- Some have lost their jobs because they couldn't control their tempers.
- Some have lost their dating or marriage relationship because they couldn't control their tempers.
- Some are a TURNOFF to everyone they meet because they can't control their tempers.
- People with hot-tempers lose all sense of rationale.
- People with hot-tempers tend to act before they think.
- People with hot tempers usually are malicious with their words.
- People with hot tempers leave a lot of destruction throughout the pathways of their lives.

My constant prayer to God is, "GIVE ME SELF-CONTROL." I don't desire to go through life hurting other people simply because I allow my temper to get the best of me.

King Solomon argues that HOT-TEMPERS LEAD TO ALL KINDS OF SINS SUCH AS:

- ARGUING
- CUSSING
- FIGHTING
- ABUSE
- VIOLENCE
- DEATH

In the heat of the moment, a hot-tempered person can throw his or her life away in a matter of seconds. Senseless killings have taken place because some individuals could not bring their TEMPERS UNDER CONTROL.

FOUR POWERFUL REASONS ARE GIVEN AS TO WHY WE NEED TO CONTROL OUR TEMPERS.

1) **OUR TEMPERS SET THE STAGE FOR OUR DAY.**
2) **OUR TEMPERS IMPACT THE ENTIRE ATMOSPHERE AROUND US.**
3) **OUR TEMPERS CAN CAUSE US T O MISS OUT ON GREAT OPPORTUNITIES IN LIFE**
4) **OUR TEMPERS CAN CAUSE OTHERS TO DISTANCE THEMSELVES FROM US.**

PERSONAL NOTES:

Chapter 15

GET RID OF THE WEIGHT

Proverbs 27:3 - *"A stone is heavy and sand is weighty, but the resentment caused by a fool is heavier than both."*

> **PROFOUND STATEMENT #25 - RESENTMENT CAN BECOME INTERNALLY TOXIC IMPACTING EVERY SYSTEM WITHIN YOUR BODY.**

Resentment is stored up anger, bitterness, hatred, and dislike toward another person.

King Solomon admonishes us to PURGE OUR SYSTEM OF RESENTMENT. He argues, RESENTMENT IS A HEAVY WEIGHT TO CARRY. He compares carrying the weight of resentment to a heavy stone or bags of sands. He argues RESENTMENT IS A WEIGHT THAT WILL ULTIMATELY BREAK US or DESTROY US!

An alarming statement is made in this proverb - RESENTMENT WITHIN US IS CAUSED BY A FOOL.

Before you allow RESENTMENT TO CONSUME YOU, THINK OF ITS ORIGIN. It is understandable why you might FEEL you have the RIGHT to harbor resentment in your heart against someone else.

- You have been scarred.
- You have been manipulated.
- You have been mishandled.
- You have been lied to.

- You have been used.
- You have been gravely disrespected.
- You have been pushed to a strange place.

However, the bigger question still remains - "IS IT WORTH IT TO HOLD ON TO RESENTMENT WHEN THE REAL DAMAGE IS BEING DONE TO YOU?" When you choose to hold on to resentment, you are not hurting the person who has caused HURTS within your life. The longer you hold on to resentment, you HEAP HURT UPON YOURSELF.

- You become toxic.
- You become filled with bitterness.
- You allow anger to eat away at you.

GET RID OF RESENTMENT BEFORE IT GETS THE BEST OF YOU!

You owe it to yourself to be the BEST YOU CAN BE EVERYDAY.

- Stop allowing people to unsettle you.
- Stop allowing people to steal the joy out of your day.
- Stop allowing people to take control of your emotions.
- Stop allowing people to make you act out of character.

PROFOUND STATEMENT #26 - WHEN YOU CAVE IN TO RESENTMENT, YOU HAVE ALLOWED SOMEONE ELSE TO GAIN CONTROL OF YOUR EMOTIONS.

You are being given SPECIAL PERMISSION to have a PRIVATE FUNERAL SERVICE for RESENTMENT. Take it to the CEMETERY and BURY IT. GIVE THE COMMITTAL SERVICE TO RESENTMENT. Send resentment back to the

PIT OF HELL from which it evolves. BID FAREWELL to this UGLY WEIGHT that has IMPRISONED you for a countless number of your years. ENJOY YOUR FIRST DAY OF NEW FRESH FREEDOM.

PROFOUND STATEMENT #27 - IF YOU FEED RESENTMENT, IT WILL CONTINUE TO GROW. IF YOU STARVE RESENTEMENT, IT WILL EVENTUALLY WITHER UP AND DIE.

RESENTMENT DOES 4 MAJOR THINGS.

1) RESENTMENT STEALS YOUR FOCUS.
2) RESENTMENT HINDERS YOU FROM MOVING ON WITH THE REST OF YOUR LIFE.
3) RESENTMENT GETS IN THE WAY OF YOUR PRAYER LIFE BY CAUSING YOUR PRAYERS NOT TO BE HEARD.
4) RESENTMENT POISONS YOU INTERNALLY.

PERSONAL NOTES:

Chapter 16

PUT A FILTER ON IT

Proverbs 10:19 - *"Don't talk too much, for it fosters sin. Be sensitive and turn off the flow."*

King Solomon addresses an issue prevalent among the human race. He emphasizes the importance of keeping a check on our conversations. In our **SELF-REFLECTIONS** we should ask, "WHAT IMPRESSIONS DO OTHERS HAVE OF US ONCE WE FINISH SPEAKING?"

An **UNFILTERED CONVERSATION** can become problematic for the speaker and all the listeners. Some people talk simply for the sake of hearing their own voice.

- They speak to be seen.
- They speak as though they are resident experts in every area.
- They speak to be impressive, but often end up frustrating everybody around them.

Sometimes the BEST PRACTICE is SILENCE. Many people could use a CENSOR BUZZER or FILTER over their mouths so that whenever they begin to speak something inappropriate, their words can be BLOCKED BY A SERIES OF BEEPS!

The best lesson is to STOP and THINK before we allow words to come GUSHING OUT OF OUR MOUTHS!

King Solomon addresses the need to bring our conversations under control. My daily prayer to the Lord is,

"GUARD THE FLOW OF WORDS COMING FROM MY MOUTH." People often ask, "Why are you so quiet?" "Why aren't you saying anything?" "I know you have something to contribute?" Oftentimes I sit in silence because I am attempting to FILTER BEFORE I SPEAK. Many people are not saying much of anything, but they just enjoy hearing themselves talk.

PROFOUND STATEMENT #28 - PEOPLE DON'T KNOW WHAT YOU ARE THINKING UNTIL YOU OPEN YOUR MOUTH. AT THAT POINT YOU REMOVE ANY SUSPENSE.

Good wholesome conversations should be embraced, but King Solomon argues that sometimes people talk too much and it leads to sin. The bible teaches us TO BE QUICK TO LISTEN and SLOW TO SPEAK (James 1:19).

We must CONDUCT MOUTH FILTER CHECKS DAILY.

- As long as we are talking to build others, keep the conversations flowing!
- As long as we are talking about the Word, keep the conversations going!
- As long as we are inspiring others, keep the conversations flowing!

However, when our conversations start to take on an UNHEALTHY NATURE, we need to put them to rest.

The bible teaches that cursing and blessings should not flow out of the same mouth (James 3:10). You have been in the presence of people who are talking SPIRITUAL one moment and then they are CUSSING the very next moment. If they are not cussing, they are BELITTLING and DEGRADING other people.

King Solomon admonishes us to BE SENSITIVE about the MOUTH FLOW! I don't want my life to become a STUMBLING BLOCK TO OTHERS; therefore, I am SELECTIVE ABOUT MY CONVERSATIONS.

Whenever we open our mouths, we have to be cognizant of the TENDER EARS who are listening. My grandson can be riding in the truck with me when I receive an incoming call. He appears to be heavily engaged in his video games. However, when the call is over, he can turn around and repeat my entire phone conversation almost VERBATIM. He is IMPRESSIONABLE; therefore, I have to guard my conversations at all times.

Parents often use CHOICE WORDS in front of their children and those same words end up on school grounds and church campuses. The children only repeat what they have heard spoken in their ears.

HOLDING OURSELVES ACCOUNTABLE FOR OUR WORDS is a daily commitment. Some folk TALK, TALK, and TALK, but do not know how to TURN OFF THEIR **TALKING VALVE!**

King Solomon admonishes us to know when to **END THE FLOW COMING FROM OUR MOUTHS!**

Two important questions we must ponder.

QUESTION 1- What do you spend most of your day talking about?

QUESTION 2- Are you proud of your overall conversations?

GET CONTROL OF WHAT IS **POURING**, **SPOUTING**, and **OVERFLOWING** OUT OF YOUR MOUTH!

FIVE THINGS WE MUST REMEMBER ABOUT OUR CONVERSATIONS

1) **OUR CONVERSATIONS WILL EITHER BUILD OR BREAK OTHERS.**
2) **OUR CONVERSATIONS WILL EITHER STRENGTHEN OR WEAKEN OUR CHRISTIAN WITNESS.**
3) **OUR CONVERSATIONS WILL EITHER GLORIFY OR BRING SHAME TO THE LORD.**
4) **OUR CONVERSATIONS WILL EITHER DRAW OTHERS TO CHRIST OR PUSH THEM AWAY FROM HIM.**
5) **OUR CONVERSATIONS WILL EITHER PROMOTE GODLINESS OR SIN.**

FILTER THE CONVERSATIONS!

PERSONAL NOTES:

Chapter 17

DON'T HIT THAT SNOOZE BUTTON AGAIN

Proverbs 6:6-11 - *"Take a lesson from the ants, you lazybones. Learn from their ways and be wise. Even though they have no prince, governor, or ruler to make them work, 8) they labor hard all summer, gathering food for the winter. 9) But you lazybones, how long will you sleep? When will you wake up? I want you to learn this lesson: 10) A little extra sleep, a little more slumber, a little folding of the hands to get rest—11) and poverty will pounce on you like a bandit; scarcity will attack you like an armed robber."*

The cliché - "THE EARLY BIRD GETS THE WORM" is very applicable to this proverb. The explanation given for this saying in the Wiktionary states, "Whoever arrives first has the best chance of success; some opportunities are only available to the first competitors.

I have entitled this Chapter, '**DON'T HIT THAT SNOOZE BUTTON AGAIN"** simply because so many people are missing out on great opportunities due to their FAILURE TO GET UP AND ACT IMMEDIATELY.

Permit me to admonish you not to go through life as a HOARDER! A hoarder spends an entire lifetime collecting stuff. A hoarder is a daily collector of material things. Hoarders are persons who stash away everything they get their hands upon. They are MISERS; therefore, they never enjoy any of their stuff. They just pile stuff up on top of stuff.

MAINTAIN A WHOLESOME BALANCE. KNOW WHEN TO COLLECT and KNOW WHEN TO DISTRIBUTE! Don't spend your entire life accumulating stuff and then miss the opportunity to enjoy any of it. Everything you acquire is TRANSIENT. LIFE IS MEANT TO BE LIVED and ENJOYED!

King Solomon addresses a bigger issue facing adults and youth. He argues all of us would be wise to study the ants and glean from them. ANTS are wise insects and when carefully studied, they provide us with some GREAT ECONOMIC LESSONS.

- Ants understand the **CONCEPTS OF SUPPLY** and **DEMAND** better than most human beings.
- Ants understand the **CONCEPT OF SCARCITY!**
- Ants understand the **CONCEPTS OF SAVINGS** and **INVESTINGS!**
- Ants understand the **CONCEPT OF ESTABLISHING A BACKUP OR CONTINGENCY PLAN!**

Unfortunately, the AVERAGE INDIVIDUALS don't have **CONTINGENCY PLANS IN PLACE.** If we have not learned any other lesson from COVID-19, we have learned the importance of preparing for **RAINY DAYS.**

It is LUDICROUS to prepare for HARD TIMES during the time of a **FAMINE.** We must prepare for FAMINE in the time of PROSPERITY.

The outbreak of COVID-19 left many families scrambling and scrounging trying to make ends meet. The first two weeks of UNEMPLOYMENT had so many pondering over how they were going to survive. American households became very vulnerable. Every household felt the crunch as businesses started to layoff and shutdown.

My mother was my first **ECON TEACHER**. She didn't teach me to be **STINGY** and **TIGHT-FISTED**, but she taught me how to live **WISE** and **CONSERVATIVE.** She taught me about the value of **MONEY** and **SPENDING.**

PROFOUND STATEMENT #29 - DON'T SPEND ALL OF YOUR MONEY INVESTING IN OTHER PEOPLES' DREAMS UNTIL YOU FORGET TO SECURE YOUR OWN DREAMS.

The admonition is for us not to go through life MAKING A FORTUNE, and then get to the end of our careers and have nothing to show for it.

The present generation makes far more money than our ancestors ever dreamed of making, but they have LESS TO SHOW FOR IT.

We should ascribe to the following practices:

- The goal is not to MAKE ALL WE CAN and SPEND ALL WE MAKE.
- The goal is to work ourselves out of debt.
- The goal is to free ourselves from the enslavement of a 9 to 5 Job!
- The goal should be to work our way into a comfortable retirement.
- The goal should be to EXERCISE GREATER SPENDING POWER WITHOUT being tied to high interest credit cards!
- The goal should be to have the FINANCIAL FREEDOM to enjoy some of the finer things of life such as travelling and exploring the world.
- The goal should be to leave an inheritance for our children to help them get a FAIR START IN LIFE!

We are admonished to **WORK HARD NOW** and to **REST EASY LATER!** If we don't INVEST and SPEND WISELY, we will set ourselves up for a LIFETIME OF STRUGGLE.

Let's applaud the **ENTREPRENUERSHIP EVOLVING** within our children. Don't crush them just because they HAVE A PASSION TO PURSUE A DIFFERENT PATH FROM THE ONE WE HAD ENVISIONED FOR THEM. When our children have dreams, passions, and aspirations, guide the PROCESSES, but also SUPPORT THEIR PLANS. We can FORCE THEM TO BE MISERABLE and FAILURES when we downplay their PASSIONS!

King Solomon advises us to study the ANTS.

- They are early risers!
- They have no supervisors!
- They work in teams!
- They prepare for the winter during the summer!
- They grab up all the crumbs they can while the crumbs are available!
- They often beat the birds and the rest of nature up as they strategically grab food and transport it to their stockpiles.

When the SEASONS CHANGE, THE ANTS ARE PREPARED FOR SURVIVAL. They don't fret seasons because they adequately prepare themselves.

King Solomon advises young people and adults not to **SLEEP OPPORTUNITIES AWAY**. We have to CHASE OPPORTUNITIES WHILE THEY ARE SET BEFORE US.

- When we continue to hit the snooze button,
- When we continue to sit around hoping a job is going to just land in our laps,

- When we don't brush up on our soft skills,
- When we make excuses about why we are not acting,
- When we sit around blaming everybody else for our downfalls and misfortunes in life,

We are setting ourselves up for POVERTY.

When I was a pre-teen, I would rise up early in the morning and go throughout the neighborhood soliciting different families for the opportunity to mow their lawns. I would rise up at the crack of dawn because I wanted to get ahead of everybody else and also beat the heat. On many occasions, I would be fortunate enough to mow or rake two or three yards within the same week.

My personal ECON TEACHER taught me to **save a portion of everything I earned.** At early age, I understood the POWER OF SAVING!

King Solomon argues that each time a person decides to get another hour of sleep, SCARCITY and POVERTY will pounce upon them.

The late Rev. Joe Louis Sweet, Jr. admonished me when I started my first job in public education to make sure **I PAY MYSELF OUT OF EVERY PAYCHECK**. He said to me, "If you are not going to pay yourself, then you don't need to work." Therefore, on every payday beginning in August 1997, I paid myself monthly through savings and investments.

SEVERAL LESSONS NEED TO BE TAKEN AWAY FROM THIS CHAPTER IF YOU WANT TO BE ECONOMICALLY EMPOWERED:

LESSON 1 - MAKE A DISTINCTION BETWEEN SPENDING, SAVINGS, AND INVESTMENTS. (SAVINGS AND INVESTMENTS ARE NOT MEANT TO BE TOUCHED).

LESSON 2 - UNDERSTAND AN INCREASE ON THE JOB DOES NOT EQUATE TO MORE SPENDING. IT'S AN OPPORTUNITY TO BUILD YOUR NEST EGG OR FUTURE SAVINGS.

LESSON 3 - LEARN TO LIVE WITHIN YOUR MEANS. OVEREXTENDING YOURSELF WILL KEEP YOU IN FINANCIAL BONDAGE.

LESSON 4 - REMEMBER SAVINGS/INVESTMENT IS A MINDSET. IF YOU CAN'T AFFORD TO SAVE, YOU CAN'T AFFORD EAT OUT, GO TO A MOVIE, AND SPLURGE EVERY MONTH.

LESSON 5 - EVALUATE YOUR MONTHLY SPENDING! KNOW WHERE YOUR DOLLARS ARE GOING!

LESSON 6 - DON'T TRY TO LIVE LIKE THE JONESES. YOUR CIRCUMSTANCES ARE UNIQUE TO YOU.

LESSON 7 - INCREASE YOUR INVESTMENTS AS OPPORTUNITIES AFFORD THEMSELVES.

LESSON 8 - ENTERTAINING GUEST WITHIN YOUR HOMES SHOULD BE DONE IN MODERATION. THOSE SMALL EVENTS BECOME COSTLY.

LESSON 9 - GIVE TO OTHERS AS YOU ARE PROMPTED BECAUSE IT WILL FREE YOU FROM GREED.

LESSON 10 - TREAT YOURSELF OCCASIONALLY AS YOU ACCOMPLISH YOUR FINANCIAL GOALS.

LESSON 11- STAY AWAY FROM HIGH INTEREST RATE CREDIT CARDS. PAY THEM OFF MONTHLY IF POSSIBLE. USE CASH OR DEBIT CARDS AS MUCH AS POSSIBLE.

LESSON 12- PAY DEBT AND USE FUNDS FOR MORE INVESTMENTS.

LESSON 13- SACRIFICE - DON'T DEVIATE FROM YOUR PLAN TO FINANCIAL SUCCESS!

ECONOMIC EMPOWERMENT is a must. It frees you to be yourself and it gives you a VOICE.

PERSONAL NOTES:

Chapter 18

IGNORE THE VOICES OF YOUR HATERS

Proverbs 12:19 - *"Truth stands the test of time, lies are soon exposed."*

Ignore the Voices of Your Haters is a chapter birthed out of personal pain and attacks. The nuggets shared in this section are designed to EMPOWER individuals who have been VICTIMS OF MALICIOUS LIES and ATTACKS.

Throughout the course of my journey in ministry and in public education, I have countless firsthand experiences I could share, but the goal is simply to ENLIGHTEN others on how to MANEUVER YOUR WAY THROUGH THE PROCESS.

King Solomon encourages us through this proverb by reminding us that WE CAN RECOVER FROM THE LIES OF OUR HATERS. My admonition to you is, "DON'T ALLOW LIES TO BREAK YOU, BUT RISE ABOVE THEM."

Oftentimes you will find yourself the VICTIM OF A LIE. For no apparent reason, a group of haters or jealous-hearted individuals will conjure up a lie on you and then circulate it with the hopes of DISCREDITING YOU! When a lie is unleashed, the goal is for the lie to GAIN MOMENTUM.

MOVERS and SHAKERS are usually the PRIMARY TARGETS of lies. Persons of great influence who are making a positive difference have to constantly BRACE FOR THE IMPACT OF MALICIOUS ONSLAUGHTS! **Unfortunately, liars are usually intimidated by your success and they fear** your next move because they know it is going to be **PHENOMENAL!**

CRITICAL QUESTION- WHY ARE YOU ALLOWING A LYING TONGUE TO SET THE TONE FOR YOUR DAY?

Keep lying tongues out of your ears. Liars are miserable and strive to entangle or drag as many as possible into their UGLY WEB! I am usually not as disturbed by the words of the liar as I am about the persons who are QUICK TO BELIEVE THE LIES SPOKEN ABOUT US. Some folk will even join in with the liars by voicing their opinions about us once a lie is IGNITED.

Because LYING SPIRITS are prevalent in the earth, we have to learn how to deal with them without becoming UNGLUED.

King Solomon basically admonishes us to recognize no matter how POPULAR A LIE becomes you can BOUNCE BACK FROM IT because TRUTH WILL ALWAYS PREVAIL! None of us are exempt from lies. All of us will occasionally find our REPUTATION, GOOD NAME, and CHARACTER TARNISHED by liars.

GET OVER THE SHOCK FACTOR-YOU ARE NOT THE FIRST VICTIM OF A LYING SPIRIT AND YOU WILL NOT BE THE LAST. Jesus had to confront lying spirits during His time on earth. He admonishes us to recognize that if He was hated, lied on, mistreated, or called all kinds of names, we can EXPECT TO EXPERIENCE SOME OF THE SAME FORMS OF ATTACKS.

The Word of God teaches us several things that give us comfort and confidence during our attacks.

First, we understand that NO WEAPON TURNED OR FORMED AGAINST US SHALL PROSPER. THE LORD WILL SLIENCE EVERY VOICE RAISED UP TO ACCUSE US (Isaiah 54:17). We will prevail or come out victorious in every incident.

Second, we understand THINGS MEANT TO DO US EVIL WILL WORK OUT FOR OUR GOOD (Genesis 50:20).

Third, we must recognize WHEN GOD IS FOR US, HE IS MORE THAN THE WHOLE WORLD AGAINST US (Romans 8:31). If the Lord is on our side, we are already on the winning team.

Admittedly, nobody enjoys being the victim of lies because we can be scarred in the process.

King Solomon admonishes us to recognize that the truth about us will SHINE EVEN IN THE MIDST OF THE ATTACKS BEING LAUNCHED AGAINST US. God will expose every liar. A lying spirit does not sit well with God. The bible teaches, "He that works deceit shall not dwell within my house: he that tells lies shall not tarry in my sight" (Psalm 101:7). God doesn't even enjoy the presence of a liar.

The most difficult kind of liar to deal with is the one who laughs in your face, but puts a dagger in your back.

Some folk are professional liars. They pride themselves on lying on everybody about everything. However, their RECKONING DAY IS COMING!

When you cross the paths of liars, you can give the following responses:

- Pray for them because they are miserable and desire for others to be miserable as well.

- Maintain your strong integrity.
- Keep your head lifted up.
- Pity the liars because they are in bad shape.
- Wait for your victory to manifest itself above the lies broadcasted about you.

WE MUST AVOID 5 DEADLY MISTAKES WHEN DEALING WITH LIARS.

MISTAKE #1 - WE OFTEN TRY TO DEFEND WHAT THE LIARS HAVE SPOKEN ABOUT US (No defense is necessary).

MISTAKE #2 - WE OFTEN ALLOW THE LIES TO BREAK US AND STEAL OUR JOY.

MISTAKE #3 - WE OFTEN ALLOW LIES TO CAUSE US TO BECOME BITTER.

MISTAKE #4 - WE OFTEN ALLOW LIES TO DERAIL OUR FOCUS!

MISTAKE #5 - WE OFTEN ALLOW LIES TO ROB US OF OUR PEACEFUL SLEEP.

King Solomon declares, LIES HAVE NO POWER OVER YOU. Don't walk around acting like a **VICTIM**, but praise GOD for every **VICTORY PRE-ORDAINED** on your behalf. You will come through the lies stronger, wiser, and better equipped to minister to others.

PERSONAL NOTES:

Chapter 19

HOLD ON TO YOUR LOVER

Proverbs 21:19 - *"It is better to live alone in the desert than with a crabby, complaining wife."*

I shared this proverb during our morning conference call on Thursday, July 2, 2020 prior to heading to the track to walk. By the time I reached the college to walk, a senior member of my congregation had sent me this hilarious lengthy text message in response to the morning devotional. I asked for her permission to share the text message in my book and it stated:

"Good Morning again Pastor. I just had to tell you this. That proverb got me. Not only did I turn it over to God and sealed my lips, but I packed my luggage and called the MOVERS. I didn't move to the desert, but I MOVED. I didn't take everything (just most of it). Have a blessed day." **– Minnie Gross.** The text message was followed by a lot of smiley face emojis.

In order to appreciate the comments above, you have to understand the context of my message to the group during our morning devotional. I admonished the group not to go through life being a **NAGGER!**

I admonished the group not to spend their entire lives COMPLAINING. I reminded the morning prayer group that whenever they seek the good in their mates or spouses, the good will be seen. However, I also shared whenever they search for the **FLAWS** in their spouses or significant others, that FLAWS would become **GLARING IN NATURE**.

Some people are involved in relationships, but they make one grave mistake that usually ends up driving the other person away. **They POSSESS THE SPIRIT OF NAGGER!**

King Solomon argues it is miserable to live under the same roof with someone who complains about everything. The quickest way to end a relationship is to LIVE THE LIFE OFA NAGGER.

PROFOUND STATEMENT #30 – SOME FOLK COMPLAIN ABOUT NOT HAVING. ONCE THEY ACQUIRE WHAT THEY SAY THEY DIDN'T HAVE, THEY START COMPLAINING ABOUT NOT HAVING ENOUGH OF IT.

I do not know how vested you are in your relationship, but I need teach you some tips to ensure you do your part TO HOLD ON TO YOUR LOVER!

- Recognize all relationships are flawed.
- Recognize all relationships are a work in progress.
- Remember your responsibility is to build your partner or mate.
- Refrain from publicly embarrassing your mate.
- Reassure your mate you are his or her strongest accountability partner.
- Remove the barriers that prevent your mate from wanting to communicate with you.
- Raise the bar of expectation as it relates to your trust and commitment for each other.

- Resolve not to SELF-SABOTAGE your relationship with **harsh** and **stinging words.**
- Reflect upon your own struggles and flaws within the relationship.
- Restore and forgive your partner beyond the hurt of the past.
- Release the anger you have inside of you in a wholesome manner.
- Respect the views of your spouse or significant other.

THE GREAT MYTH – NAGGING CAN CHANGE ANOTHER PERSON.

We have fooled ourselves into thinking the more we nag the other person, the greater our chances become to FOSTER CHANGE.

THE REALITY CHECK- WE DON'T POSSESS THE POWER TO CHANGE OTHER PEOPLE.

- If people want to drink, they are going to drink.
- If people want to be degrading, they are going to degrade you and others.
- If people want to smoke, you cannot force them to quit.
- If people are unmotivated, you can't force them to have a strong determination.

PROFOUND STATEMENT #31 - REAL CHANGE CAN ONLY OCCUR WITHIN THE LIVES OF INDIVIDUALS WHEN THEY ARE WILLING TO DO THE WORK.

The habits, behaviors, and quirks you see while dating and dining your significant other are more than likely to be the same actions you will experience when you give your hand to the person in marriage. **PUTTING A RING ON A FINGER IS NOT A MAGICAL WAND!** Both parties involved in the relationship must continue to invest in themselves and their soul mate.

- You can pray for your partner.
- You can bring matters to your partner's attention.
- You can support your partner in his or her struggles.
- You can provide accountability for your partner.

However, you do not possess the **POWER TO GIVE SOMEONE ELSE AN INTERNAL MAKEOVER!**

Multiple NEGATIVE ACTIONS accompany NAGGING!

- Nagging will anger you.
- Nagging will make you feel defeated.
- Nagging will drive you to a bitter place.
- Nagging will cause you to ACT OUT OF CHARACTER.
- Nagging will frustrate the other party.
- Nagging will push the other person farther away from you.
- Nagging will cause the other person to put up walls thus tearing down future communication opportunities.

When you have tried to help your spouse or dating counterpart and the person is not RECEPTIVE to the help being offered, you have to know when to STEP BACK! The most difficult practice for us is that of **PUTTING A SEAL ON OUR LIPS and TAKING THE PERSON TO GOD IN PRAYER.**

We don't possess the POWER TO FIX OTHERS. The worst tactic you can employ as you are trying to hold on to your lover is CONSTANT NAGGING.

King Solomon says an EXTENDED TRIP or VACATION to the DESERT would be better than sitting on the COUCH next to someone who is a PROFESSIONAL COMPLAINER.

Meditate on the principles taught in this chapter and determine how you can strengthen your own relationship. If you do the work within your life, it will grant you the patience and wisdom you need to HELP your partner through the process.

We can only BECOME BETTER OURSELVES.

THE FOLLOWING FIVE REASONS ARE GIVEN AS TO WHY WE OUGHT TO AVOID NAGGING:

1) **A NAGGER IS OFTEN PERSONALLY DISSATISFIED.**
2) **A NAGGER SELDOM DOES SELF-REFLECTION TO DETERMINE HIS OR HER CONTRIBUTIONS TO ISSUES EXISTING WITHIN THE RELATIONSHIP ISSUES.**
3) **A NAGGER FALSELY BELIEVES THAT ARUGING AND CONSTANT VERBAL TORTURE WILL BRING ABOUT IMMEDIATE CHANGE.**
4) **A NAGGER DOES NOT RECOGNIZE THE WASTED ENERGY BEING USED TO TRY TO DETHRONE DEEPLY-ROOTED MINDSETS.**
5) **A NAGGER MISSES OUT ON THE OPPORTUNITIES TO CELEBRATE SMALL SUCCESSES WITHIN HIS OR HER PARTNER.**

PERSONAL NOTES:

Chapter 20

STEP BACK FOOL

Proverbs 29:11 - *"A fool gives full vent to anger, but a wise person quietly holds it back."*

Fools in the bible are described as irrational, out-of-control, unreasonable thinking individuals.

You will not have to wonder when you have crossed the path of a fool. Simply observe the person's **VENTING PROCESS**.

I understand the **BENEFITS OF VENTING.**

- Venting allows us to release stuff off of our chest.
- Venting allows us to emit poisonous toxins that could be detrimental to our well-being being.
- Venting allows us to expel our anger.
- Venting provides an avenue through which we can calmly express ourselves.

King Solomon does not downplay the IMPORTANCE OF VENTING. However, he admonishes us to stay away from the type of venting that is UNFILTERED.

My prayer to the Lord is – "Teach me to restrain my anger." All of us have some ANGER WAITING TO BE UNLEASED.

However, for our sake and for the well-being of others, we have a **RESPONSIBILTY TO GUARD HOW WE HANDLE OUR ANGER.** We can choose to RATIONALLY and INTELLIGENTLY ADDRESS THOSE WHO HAVE

SCARRED or WRONGED US or we can just go off without giving a thought to our words.

Built up anger causes us to be like a PRESSURE COOKER. If RELIEF is not eventually given, we will EXPLODE.

UNADDRESSED ANGER can poison our entire body systems.

- UNADDRESSED ANGER will work on our minds.
- UNADDRESSED ANGER will work on our nerves.
- UNADDRESSED ANGER will infuriate us.
- UNADDRESSED ANGER will strain our heart.
- UNADDRESSED ANGER will cause our blood pressure to be elevated.
- UNADDRESSED ANGER can cause ulcers.
- UNADDRESSED ANGER can interfere with our ability to operate with SOUND JUDGMENT.

Therefore, ANGER HAS TO BE ADDRESSED.

King Solomon says a FOOL just vents his or her anger with no regards given to the consequences.

- A fool simply explodes.
- A fool just displays anger anywhere and anytime.
- A fool doesn't worry about who gets damaged in the VENTING PROCESS.
- A fool is very careless and relentless.
- A fool will spiral out of control.

However, a **WISE PERSON** finds **WHOLESOME WAYS TO MANAGE OR EXPRESS THE ANGER.**

- Wise people don't just lash out simply because others have lashed out at them.

- Wise people don't cuss at others just because profanity has been used towards them.
- Wise people don't publicly embarrass others simply because they have been a victim of public degradation.
- Wise people don't give other people CONTROL OF THEIR EMOTIONS.

As a WISE MAN, I GET TO CHOOSE HOW TO HANDLE MY ANGER. My objective is to leave a situation better than how I found it. My goal is to model intelligence during the most intense conversations.

We must understand the following thoughts about CONTROLLING or PUTTING A LEASH ON OUR ANGER.

- Restraining our anger doesn't mean we are weak.
- Restraining our anger doesn't mean we are pushovers.
- Restraining our anger doesn't mean we haven't been scarred.
- Restraining our anger doesn't mean we don't desire to be heard.
- Restraining our anger doesn't mean we are giving the other person the upper hand.

FOUR PRACTICES WE NEED TO EMPLOY BEFORE TACKLING A SITUATION WE ARE HEATED OVER:

1) CONDUCT SOME SELF-REFLECTION. Make sure we understand the actions we may have displayed that fueled the situation.
2) MAINTAIN A CALM VOICE. A loud voice may send the wrong message of intimidation.
3) STAY IN CONTROL OF OUR WORDS. Once our words are released into the atmosphere, there is no retrieving them.

4) **RELEASE and MOVE FORWARD. Once a matter has been discussed and resolved, we have to learn to let it go.**

We cannot reason with a fool; therefore, we need to reserve that energy.

PERSONAL NOTES:

Chapter 21

RUN FROM ILL-GOTTEN GAINS

Proverbs 10:2 - *"Ill-gotten gain has no lasting value, but right living can save your life."*

> **PROFOUND STATEMENT #32 UNGODLY GAINS are often ACCOMPANIED BY A LARGE UNDESIRABLE PRICE TAG.**

Ill-gotten gain usually leads to a pathway of destruction. WORKING HARD and ACQUIRING REPUTABLE GAINS are two frowned upon statements.

The message conveyed by King Solomon in this proverb needs to be revisited by youth and adults.

CURRENT DAY MINDSET - I'VE GOT TO HAVE IT AND I MUST HAVE IT NOW!

Oftentimes, it appears as though we are raising a generation that wants something out of life for nothing. Unfortunately, the virtue of PATIENCE is no longer readily embraced.

WE MUST LEARN SEVERAL VALUES.

- We must learn the value of patience.
- We must learn the value of good work ethics.
- We must learn the value of honesty.
- We must learn the value of integrity.
- We must learn the value of saving.

- We must learn the value of starting out small and expanding.

WE MUST EMBACE CERTAIN REALITIES.

- If we've got to cheat our way to the top, it is not worth it.
- If we've got to use other people to get top, it is going to be a hard fall coming back down the ladder.
- If we've got to brown nose our way to the top, our promotions will be short-lived.
- If we have to sell drugs to get ahead, we are setting ourselves up for imprisonment.
- If we've got to embezzle our way to the top, our palace will come tumbling down.

King Solomon argues you may lay hands on wealth, properties, and stuff temporarily, but the DAY OF A GREAT FALL IS COMING.

I don't desire anything that belongs to someone else. I don't desire anything I've got to acquire by ill means. My life is covered with favor; therefore, I know I shall be blessed.

SAD STORY ENDINGS

- People have ended up serving lifetime prison sentences trying to rob their way to the top.
- People have ended up losing their lives in drug deals that went sour.
- People have ended up suffering great falls because they hurt everyone in their path in route to the top of the ladder.

King Solomon argues that if you live right, God will meet every need within your life.

"LEARNING TO CRAWL BEFORE WE WALK" is not a bad principle to embrace. It takes time to build a LIFE OF SUCCESS. We must ESTABLISH OUR PLAN and then EXECUTE THE PLAN. ILL-GAIN will serve as a SOURCE OF ENTRAPMENT for some. However, when God establishes us, we are SET FOR LIFE.

FOUR LESSONS WE NEED TO UNDERSTAND ABOUT DOING IT GOD'S WAY

1) **HE WILL SUPPLY ALL OF OUR NEEDS ACCORDING TO HIS RICHES IN GLORY (Philippians. 4:19).**
2) **HE WILL GIVE US EVERY GOOD AND PERFECT GIFT (James 1:17).**
3) **HE WILL BLESS EXCEEDINGLY ABUNDANTLY ABOVE ALL WE CAN ASK OR THINK (Eph. 3:20).**
4) **HE WILL ADD ALL WE NEED UNTO US IF WE WILL SEEK HIS FACE FIRST (Matt. 6:33).**

PERSONAL NOTES:

Chapter 22

LORD, GRANT ME WISDOM

Proverbs 9:10-12 - *"Fear of the Lord is the beginning of wisdom. Knowledge of the Holy One results in understanding.*
11) *Wisdom will multiply your days and add years to your life.*
12) *If you become wise, you will be the one to benefit. If you scorn wisdom, you will be the one to suffer."*

Wisdom is a virtue we must embrace if we desire success and longevity in life.

I could pray for a lot of other blessings, but superior to all requests is **THE PLEA FOR WISDOM!** Some people try to go through life on the merits of their own intelligence.

However, Proverbs 3:5-6 teaches us to trust the Lord with all of our heart and don't lean to our own understanding. We are encouraged to admonish the Lord in every endeavor and He will direct our path.

Most of our FAILURES are due to our UNWILLINGNESS TO SEEK THE COUNSEL OF GOD. The MAZE called LIFE is too complex to get through without God's daily guidance.

King Solomon argues that WISDOM is a virtue we must ACTIVATE within our lives. He argues that our WHOLESOME FUTURES DEPEND UPON US EMBRACING WISDOM. Our ability to please and to glorify the Lord depends upon our willingness to EMBRACE WISDOM!

WE MUST UNDERSTAND SEVERAL REALTIES.

- Without wisdom, life will be fruitless.
- Without wisdom, life will end up being one big disaster.
- Without wisdom, we will end up selling ourselves short.
- Without wisdom, we will miss out on all God has in store for us.

WE MUST RECOGNIZE THE ORIGIN OF WISDOM.

- Wisdom originates with God.
- Wisdom starts with a fear of God.
- Wisdom means a reverence for God.
- Wisdom means respect for God.
- Wisdom means a reverence for the Word of God.
- Wisdom means implementing God's Word in our daily lives.

The Word of God teaches, there is a way that seems right to man, but it ends in death. If we go through life viewing it through our own lenses, we will eventually perish.

The greatest MISTAKE I have ever made in life was that of trying to OPERATE WITHOUT GOD! I learned quickly that I couldn't do anything without Him, but all things were possible through Him. (Phil 4:13).

- Life is too turbulent without God.
- Life is too problematic without God.
- Life is too perplexed without God.

If we don't SEEK KNOWLEDGE and WISDOM from God, life will SWALLOW US UP!

King Solomon argues WISDOM will multiply our days and years in life. We can live a LONGER and MORE PRODUCTIVE LIFE if we apply wisdom.

King Solomon argues WISDOM adds benefits to our lives. However, people who scorn wisdom and ignore the Word of God will suffer greatly.

Pray daily for wisdom and it will be granted. Every decision in your life will fare better when you apply Godly wisdom. The more you walk with God and chase after His Word, the more SPIRITUALLY ENLIGHTENED you will become. WHATEVER YOU DO, NEVER PUSH ASIDE OR TURN A DEAF EAR TO GODLY WISDOM.

FOUR REASONS WISDOM HOLDS A PLACE OF VALUE WITHIN OUR LIVES.

1) **WISDOM SERVES AS OUR TOUR GUIDE OR SPIRITUAL GPS THROUGH LIFE.**
2) **WISDOM HELPS US TO KEEP A PULSE ON THE HEART OF GOD.**
3) **WISDOM BRINGS US INTO A PLACE OF BLESSINGS AND BENEFITS.**
4) **WISDOM ENABLES US TO LIVE A FULL AND PRODUCTIVE LIFE.**

PERSONAL NOTES:

Chapter 23

USE YOUR MANNERS

Proverbs 25:17 - *"Don't visit your neighbors too often, or else you will wear out your welcome."*

___

King Solomon shares with us the value of exercising common sense as it relates to visiting the homes of others. He admonishes us **NOT TO BE FREQUENT VISITORS WITHOUT THE PROPER INVITATION.**

I have learned that just because people are cordial, it doesn't mean they want us to show up on the doorstep every day. **Visit in moderation.**

King Solomon admonishes us to understand that VISITING TOO OFTEN CAN LEAD TO US WEARING OUT OUR **VISITATION PRIVILEGES.**

As a child growing up, I thought my mother was one of the strictest parents in the neighborhood. We played a lot of community games, street basketball, football, kickball, and volleyball. We engaged in games of marbles. However, at a certain time, my mother expected us to make our way towards the house.

She allowed us to play with our community friends because we all stayed next door to each other; however, she was not big on us spending the night with other people.

When we went to visit a community home, she would coach us concerning our responsibility.

- We couldn't go play and run around in the homes of other people.
- We had to sit in a designated area.
- We couldn't ask the homeowners for something to eat or drink.
- We were not allowed to sit and listen to adult conversations.
- We had to exercise politeness and manners when we were offered something. My mother trained us to say "THANK-YOU" even if we were only given a glass of water.

My mother didn't believe in us being FREQUENT VISITORS because her philosophy was that people didn't want to pull up into their driveways every day and see our faces. She taught us that a home was the place where the individuals could let their hair down and be free to do whatever they wanted. However, she believed that our constant presence within the home would IMPEDE UPON OTHERS PRIVACY.

My mother used to say, **"SHORT VISITS MAINTAIN WHOLESOME FRIENDSHIPS."**

I enjoy entertaining people. I want them to feel my love and warmth when they enter into my presence. I feel just as obligated to be a GREAT HOST as they feel about being GREAT GUESTS.

The best practice is simply to be considerate and respectful of each person's situation and circumstances.

King Solomon dittos everything my mother taught us. He argues it is alright to be neighborly. He taught it is perfectly fine to pay people an occasional visit. However, he argues too much visitation can result in your welcome being worn out.

I have lived my entire life trying to respect the **PRIVACY OF OTHERS.** Whenever a lunch or dinner invitation is extended, I go and dine for a reasonable amount of time, make light conversations, and then exit the home of the host.

Most people are very cordial and will say, "YOU ARE WELCOME HERE ANYTIME." Please don't take that literally. **You don't have a FREE PASS to show up at somebody's home anytime you desire.**

Whenever a host is expecting guests, the host needs proper time to prepare the home, the meal, and the surrounding areas. Most of us have certain days when we mop, clean, dust and do laundry. When a guest shows up unexpected, it often puts us in a bind. We suddenly find ourselves doing some quick shifting and we pray our unexpected guest doesn't have to go into the closet or ask us to see the rest of the house.

When the doorbell rings UNEXPECTEDLY, we start asking everyone in the house if guests are expected. If the response is "NO", we start to wonder in panic who is ringing the doorbell or knocking on the door.

PROFOUND STATEMENT #33 - IT IS BETTER TO EXERCISE COMMON SENSE AND MAKE A VISIT BY INVITATION RATHER THAN BEING ASKED TO LEAVE THE PREMISES.

LISTED BELOW ARE SOME COMMON SENSE PRACTICES WE NEED TO EMPLOY WHEN VISITING THE HOME OF A HOST/HOSTESS.

1) BE SURE TO VISIT BY INVITATION ONLY.

2) BE SURE TO MAINTAIN A WHOLECOME CONVERSATION DURING THE VISIT.

3) BE SURE TO SET TIME LIMITS ON YOUR VISIT.

4) BE SURE YOU EXPRESS APPRECIATION FOR YOUR HOST/HOSTESS'S ACT OF LABOR.

5) BE SURE YOU OFFER YOUR ASSISTANCE WITH SETTING THE TABLE, PREPARING AND SERVING THE MEAL, and THE CLEANUP PROCESS.

6) BE SURE YOU DON'T MAKE THE HOST/HOSTESS FEEL UNCOMFORTABLE WITHIN THEIR OWN HOME.

PERSONAL NOTES:

Chapter 24

WIN THEM OVER WITH YOUR WORDS

Proverbs 12:14 - *"People can get many good things by the words they say; the work of their hands also gives them many benefits."*

The words spoken in this proverb are gentle reminders to us of the **POWER OF OUR WORDS.**

PROFOUND STATEMENT #34 - THE USE OF OUR WORDS CAN EITHER MAKE US OR BREAK US!

Some people specialize in CHOPPING OTHER PEOPLE UP with their words. They SNAP UP everyone who crosses their path. Without even giving it a second thought, they utter the first words that come to their minds.

Sometimes, we would be wise to **TASTE OUR WORDS BEFORE WE SERVE THEM UP TO OTHERS.**

- When we speak, are people drawn to the conversations?
- When we speak, do people end up respecting or disrespecting us?
- When we speak, do we create a climate of trust?
- When we speak, do others feel comfortable enough to constructively shed insights concerning our ideas?
- When we speak, do we turn people off?
- When we speak, do our audiences readily embrace our ideas?

- When we speak, are we speaking to build comradery?

Our words have the power to bless, strengthen, and build others. Our words also have the power to sting, scar, and crush others. Our words possess the power to cause others to respond favorably or unfavorably towards us.

- If our words are kind,
- If our words are filled with compassion,
- If our words are considerate,

WE POSSESS THE POWER TO HAVE PEOPLE EATING OUT OF THE PALMS OF OUR HANDS.

On many occasions, people want to perform/do for us, but the way we APPROACH them is a TURNOFF.

- Parents need to be mindful how they speak to their children.
- Children need to be respectful when they are addressing their parents.
- Employers must be considerate and thoughtful when they are addressing their employees.
- Friends must be mindful of their tones when speaking to members of their friendship circle.

Whenever people do for us because we make them feel appreciated, valued, respected, and heard, WE GAIN SO MUCH MORE GROUND WITH THEM. We also build trusted relationships for life.

The worst practice we can engage in is that of **THROWING OUR WEIGHT AROUND TO TRY TO INTIMIDATE OTHERS THROUGH THE USE OF OUR STERN** and **HARSH WORDS.**

PROFOUND STATEMENT #35 - WE MAY GET PEOPLE TO ACT FOR US OUT OF FEAR, BUT IT DOESN'T MEAN WE ARE EFFECTIVE NOR RESPECTED.

King Solomon simply admonishes us to THINK ABOUT HOW WE SAY WHAT FLOWS OUT OF OUR MOUTHS. Words make lasting impressions. Even when we are striving to communicate effectively, our conversations are often misunderstood.

However, to be OUTRIGHT BRUTAL in our conversations is a RECIPE FOR DISASTER.

- We don't enjoy others screaming at us.
- We don't take to kindly to others talking down to us like we are not intelligent.
- We don't enjoy being talked to like a child.
- We don't enjoy others attempting to degrade us or show us up.

We must remember those thoughts as we hold conversations with others.

King Solomon says the work of our hands will get us many great things. God has gifted our hands to PRODUCE. We must put them to work on our behalf. Equally important, God has given us the ABILITY TO USE OUR SPEECH and COMMUNICATION SKILLS to FOSTER WHOLESOME RELATIONSHIPS.

If people are reluctant to have conversations with us, we need to do some SELF-REFLECTION to figure out the reasons behind their CONSTANT HESITATION and DISCOMFORT.

I pride myself on WINNING PEOPLE over through CANDID, COMPASSIONATE, and COURAGEOUS CONVERSATIONS. BUILDING LASTING RELATIONSHIPS will hinge upon your ability to COMMUNICATE IN LOVE!

SIX TIPS ARE PROVIDED TO ENSURE THAT OUR WORDS WILL BE A BLESSING AND BUILD OTHERS.

1) **CONDUCT A TASTE TEST -** If you are wise, you would not serve food to your guest without sampling it prior to their consumption of the meal. Likewise, taste your words before you serve them up.

2) **REHEARSE YOUR CONVERSATION -** When you repeatedly rehearse the conversation you plan to share with others, it not only takes the edge off of things for you, but it also allows you to anticipate certain responses so you can adequately prepare to give a SOLID REBUTTAL or CONFIRMATION.

3) **DELIVER YOUR MESSAGE WITH COMPASSION-** No matter how factual your message is, it still needs to be delivered with compassion.

4) **MONITOR YOUR TONE -** Speak softly and kindly. Don't continuously elevate your voice or else it will make you appear to be hostile or disgruntled.

5) **ASK QUESTIONS TO ENSURE THE RECEIVER HEARD THE MESSAGE YOU WERE TRYING TO CONVEY -** Even though you know what you are trying to convey, it is critical to ensure the RECEIVER heard the same thing.

6) **REFRAIN FROM SPEAKING WHEN YOU ARE EMOTIONAL or HEATED -** A wholesome, well-

intended conversation can go sour very quickly when individuals allow their emotions to get in the way. OVERHEATED CONVERSATIONS usually do more damage than good.

PERSONAL NOTES:

About the Author

(THE PERSONAL STRUGGLES)

I am humbled to be able to share my personal journey with others through the publication of this book. I give all praise, honor, and glory to God for gifting me to share my PASSION with the world.

I was born on May 7, 1966 to the late Mrs. Willie Mae Wooden and the late Mr. Arthur Dean Wooden. Unfortunately, I never shared an endearing father-son relationship with my dad, Mr. Arthur Dean Wooden. The relationship became very strained when my dad abandoned my mother leaving her with six sons and one daughter to take care of when I was around the age of five years old.

Due to the tremendous strain of trying to raise a family on her own with limited resources and less than a junior high school education, my mother fell prey to the **PUBLIC WELFARE SYSTEM**. I watched her work in pecan orchards, clean houses, shell peas, and iron clothing for other families just to keep food on our table and to keep a roof over our heads.

On many occasions after a long day of work, my mother would make it to her favorite recliner and literally collapse from exhaustion. However, as soon as the sun rose the next day, she would land back on her feet determined to make provisions for her children. Some days she would be in excruciating pain, but she kept moving just so our basic needs could be met.

As I became of age, I watched my mother's struggles and vowed I would have a much better way of life. We didn't have a lot of material things when I was growing up, **but our household was filled with love.** Although I don't desire to return to that childhood lifestyle again, I am blessed because of the love we received throughout the course of my upbringing.

My mother taught us the importance of **RESPECT.** She taught us to be **INTEGRAL.** She taught us the importance of **SAVING.** She taught us the value of **TREATING OF OTHERS** as we desired to be treated. She taught us the importance of **GOOD WORK ETHICS.**

My mother repeatedly said to us, *"IF YOU WANT SOMETHING GOOD OUT OF LIFE, YOU ARE GOING TO HAVE TO WORK HARD TO GET IT. NOTHING GOOD COMES EASY!"*

Because of this strong motherly figure, I am the man of STRENGTH and HONOR I represent today.

I was called to preach the Gospel of Jesus Christ at the age of 17. As a student in high school, I recognized I could not escape my **DIVINE MINISTRY ASSIGNMENT.** I have been preaching for over 37 years and pastoring for almost 34 years. I have been in the public education system for approximately 30 years.

I speak from the **VOICE OF EXPERIENCE!** I know the **VALUE OF PERSONAL EMPOWERMENT!** My humble upbringings taught me the importance of **PERSEVERANCE.**

I also had the honor of knowing both of my late grandfathers, John Henry Wooden and Willie James Johnson. I loved both of those men dearly. However, I was privileged to spend a tremendous amount of time with my grandad, Willie James Johnson. I watched that man work on another person's farm for more than 60 years. He started out making less than $50 dollars a week. He was elevated to $75 dollars a week after more than 20 years of service. Prior to ending his career on the farm, he was making a little under $200 a week after 60 years of service.

Driven by the personal struggles of my mother and the drenching sweat that fell daily from my grandfather's forehead, I was motivated to pursue a better way of life.

Throughout the course of my life, God has strategically placed teachers in my path who believed in me. I will never forget personalities such as **Georgia Kline, Margaret Neely, Luther Conyers, Marie Johnson, Martha Hodges, Eudora Fagg, and Pauline Love,** who believed in me when others just viewed me as another statistic in the crowd. I could write books about how each of these persons impacted my life.

As an elementary, middle, and high school student, I was granted the privilege to work at several community stores – **Red Long Bait and Tackle Shop, Henderson's Grocery**, and **Alford Grocery's**. However, the bulk of my work was at Red Long Bait and Tackle. Mr. "Red" Long and Mrs. Betty Sue Long took me and my siblings under their wings and started us on our JOURNEY TO SUCCESS! I will forever be indebted to the Long Family for opening their doors to me and my siblings. Through their kind generosity, we were able to help my struggling mom make provisions for us.

As my brothers aged, they moved on to other jobs, but my sister, Emma and I continued to work at Red Long Bait and Tackle until the store permanently closed.

My mother sat me and all my siblings down one day and shared with us how gravely important it was for us to get an education. Unfortunately, her vision was limited because she didn't have a high school diploma herself.

However, she said to each of us, **"It would make me extremely proud if each of you simply graduate from high school"**. Fortunately, her prayers were answered. We all graduated from high school as she had wished.

I possess a **strong personal inner drive** and I have always been very competitive as it related to academics. Upon graduating from Bainbridge High School as an Honor Graduate in 1986, **something inside of me just wouldn't allow me to end my educational journey with just a high school diploma. I had to have more.** Although there were no funds set aside for me to go to college, I was determined to earn some higher degrees.

I started working at Hutto Junior High School in Bainbridge Georgia in 1986 as a custodian to help pay my way through Bainbridge College where I earned my first Associate of Arts Degree in Business Education. I continued to work at Hutto as paraprofessional for three years (1989-92) to pay my way through Valdosta State College.

I never had the privilege of staying on a college campus. I would work my full-time job from 7:45 a.m. to 3:45 p.m. and then drive three nights a week for two and half years from Bainbridge to Valdosta in an effort to obtain my dual Bachelor Degrees in Marketing and Management. However, when I finally reached the finishing line, I was extremely proud of the accomplishment.

I witnessed the pride all in my mother's eyes when we returned home from my Valdosta State Graduation Ceremony. She hugged me extremely tight and the uncontrollable tears began to flow from her eyes. She could not believe the great accomplishment. She had herself a **first-time bachelor's degree son**!

In my private time, I reflected upon the journey and also shed some uncontrollable tears. I couldn't believe I had risen from being a **WELFARE RECIPIENT** to a person with dual degrees. My lovely wife, Deborah and the rest of my family members also shared in the JOY OF THE OCCASION!

After completing my degrees from Valdosta State, I enrolled in a Master's Degree Seminary Program at New Orleans Baptist and completed two and half years of study through that program at the Florida Baptist Bible College Campus in Graceville, Florida.

I eventually ran for a seat on the local school board for District 3 for Decatur County Public Schools and served from 1993-1996.

My journey in public education as a teacher started in August of 1997. Dr. Suzi Bonifay invited me to join the team of West Bainbridge Middle School as a business ed/career counselor and I soared with the West Bainbridge Middle School Eagles while completing my Master's and Specialist Degrees from Nova Southeastern University.

In 2003-2005, I served as the assistant Principal of Lillian E Williams Elementary School in Attapulgus, Georgia. In 2005-2013, I served as the Assistant Principal of Bainbridge High School. In 2013-2017, I served as the principal of Bainbridge Middle School. In 2017-2020, I served as the Assistant Superintendent of Decatur County Schools.

THE REMARKABLE DREAM unfolded itself before my very eyes. I went from **PUSHING A BROOM AS A**

CUSTODIAN in 1986 to **RETIRING as ASSISTANT SUPERINTENDENT OF DECATUR COUNTY PUBLIC SCHOOLS in June of 2020.** I have experienced an AMAZING and LIFE-CHANGING JOURNEY. I have stories to tell and books to write about my journey in public education and ministry so stay tuned.

My personal philosophy is - "**YOU CAN ALLOW LIFE'S BITTER CIRCUMSTANCES TO BREAK YOU OR TO MAKE YOU BETTER.**" I choose to become BETTER!

The writing of this book is only the first of many publications I will strive to put into print. I have a passion for PREACHING and WRITING, but more importantly, I possess a longing desire to **POSITIVELY IMPACT THE LIVES OF OTHER PEOPLE ONE LIFE AT A TIME!**

My dreams and aspirations center around sharing the Word of God with individuals to **ENRICH, EMPOWER, ENLIGHTEN,** and **ENCOURAGE** them on their journeys through life. Throughout the course of my life, I have dreamed of being able to sit down and compile all of my sermons, speeches, and plays into a printable form to share them with the world. It has never been my desire to **TAKE GREAT TALENT TO THE GRAVE.**

As author of UNCENSORED CONVERSATIONS, I pray your journey through life be as remarkable and fulfilling as my journey has been.

TESTIMONIALS FROM PEOPLE WHO SHARE PRAYER CALLS!

"Prayer time is a mighty blessing. I am always uplifted. Just enough is shared to get you energized and focused on God and His Word…" – **Janet Crawford**

"I can't speak for anyone else, but the morning sessions have become a part of the spiritual growth I am experiencing." – **Tiffany Hall**

"The brief empowering messages bring hope for each day during this Pandemic. More and more people are suffering from Mental Health issues because they do not see an end to all the issues that are going on throughout the world." – **Dianne Washington**

"God has used you to put a different outlook on His Word and for that I feel truly blessed." - **Pat Greene**

"God always ministers to me through you on issues I've never disclosed. The messages are truly a blessing to the body of Christ." – **Sylvia Jacobs**

"God's Word will not go out and return void. It has enriched me and helped others. The morning prayer sessions are very inspirational." - **Lady Delores Burns**

"I wish you only knew how much the morning devotionals have meant to me. They have given me such inspiration. Many lives are being touched." - **Constance Hamilton**

"The morning devotionals are opening our eyes and ears to God's Words and giving us a better understanding of God and His Power." - **Wanda Brown**

"I think the morning sessions are really helping us. I know I am becoming better. The JUMPSTART WORD is exactly what we need to empower our day!" - **Deborah Wooden**

"It's nice to be able to connect with everyone every morning and your energy gets us going. I take notes every morning and use them to guide my actions throughout the day." – **Josette Beard**

"Every day the Word has met me in my present circumstances." - **Pauletta Malone**

I received countless other positive comments through a survey I conducted on July 10, 2020. Just wanted to share a few with you and encourage you to become a part of our morning prayer time via Conference Calls (425-436-6389: Access Code 305278). Join us and be blessed!

Afterthought

I hope these candid, thought-provoking, and **UNCENSORED CONVERSATIONS** THROUGH THE BOOK OF PROVERBS have blessed each of you as I much as I have enjoyed sharing them.

I hope you will never view THE BOOK OF PROVERBS through the same SPIRITUAL LENSES! When you read the rest of the proverbs, approach them with an opened mind as the Holy Spirit speaks to you concerning your own life.

You owe it to yourself and to the people you love to strive to live your **BEST LIFE!** Today can mark the start of a **FRESH BEGINNING** for you. Accept the challenge. Exercise Godly wisdom and watch your life **CHANGE FOR THE BETTER!**

You have been **EMPOWERED TO AVOID** many of the **PITFALLS** that have caused others to stumble. You were **BOLD** enough to take the journey through this book. Encourage others to take the **LEAP OF FAITH.**

This book was birthed in me through the POWER OF THE HOLY SPIRIT; therefore, I know lives will be CHANGED!

SUGGESTED/RECOMMENDED READINGS

Burkett, Larry. *The Complete Financial Guide for Young Couples: A Lifetime Approach to Spending, Saving, and Investing*. United States: Victor Books, 1993.

Dunn, Ronald. *Don't just Stand there, Pray Something: The Incredible Power of Intercessory Prayer*. Nashville, TN. Thomas Nelson Publishers, 1992.

Jakes, T. D. Naked and Not Ashamed: We've Been Afraid to Reveal What God Longs to Heal. Shippenburg, PA. Treasure House, 1995.

Jeremiah, David. *Slaying the Giants in Your Life: You Can Win the Battle and Live Victoriously*. Nashville, TN. W Publishing Group, 2001.

Meyers, Joyce. *Battlefield of the Mind: Winning the Battle in Your Mind*. New York, NY: Warner Faith, 2002.

Osteen, Joel. *Your Best Life Ever: 7 Steps to Living at Your Full Potential*. New York, NY. Warner Faith, 2004.

Perkins, Bill. *Six Battles Every Man Must Win...and the Ancient Secrets You'll Need to Win*. Wheaton, Illinois: Tyndale House Publishers, Inc. 200

CPSIA information can be obtained
at www.ICGtesting.com
Printed in the USA
BVHW080935151020
591023BV00011B/880

9 781087 912134